Alternative English

Literature Coursework 16–19

Colin Swatridge

Stanley Thornes (Publishers) Ltd

Text © Colin Swatridge 1989
Original line illustrations © Stanley Thornes (Publishers) Ltd 1989

All rights reserved. No part of this publication may be reproduced or transmitted in any form or by any means, electronic or mechanical, including photocopy, recording, or any information storage and retrieval system, without permission in writing from the publisher or under licence from the Copyright Licensing Agency Limited. Further details of such licences (for reprographic reproduction) may be obtained from the Copyright Licensing Agency Limited, of 33–4 Alfred Place, London WC1E 7DP.

First published in 1989 by:
Stanley Thornes (Publishers) Ltd
Old Station Drive
Leckhampton
CHELTENHAM GL53 0DN
England

British Library Cataloguing in Publication Data
Swatridge, Colin
 Alternative English.
 1. Great Britain. Secondary Schools. Curriculum subjects: English literature. Criticism. Teaching
 I. Title
 820'.7'1241

ISBN 0-7487-0065-X

Typeset by Tech-Set, Gateshead, Tyne & Wear
Printed and bound in Great Britain at The Bath Press, Avon

CONTENTS

Preface	v
Acknowledgements	vii
Introduction	ix
One Novels and short stories	**1**
What is a novel?	1
What is a short story?	3
What do we look for in a novel?	3
How might one write about a novel?	8
1 Another point of view L. P. Hartley: *The Go-Between*	8
2 A letter from one character to another Jane Austen: *Northanger Abbey*	11
3 An alternative ending Katherine Mansfield: *Selected Stories*	14
4 The film of the book E. M. Forster: *A Passage to India*	16
5 Dramatisation Charles Dickens: *Hard Times*	19
6 The writer's life and work James Joyce: *Dubliners*	21
7 The writer's 'message' George Orwell: *Nineteen Eighty-Four* F. Scott Fitzgerald: *The Great Gatsby*	24
8 A line to the author Ngugi Wa Thiongo: *Petals of Blood*	26
Two Plays	**29**
What is a play?	29
What do we look for in a play?	32
How might one write about a play?	37
1 Adding a scene Harold Pinter: *The Caretaker*	37
2 The significance of a title Arthur Miller: *Death of a Salesman*	39
3 Interview with an actor William Shakespeare: *Measure for Measure*	42
4 A first-night review Ben Jonson: *Volpone*	44
5 Radio to stage Dylan Thomas: *Under Milk Wood*	48
6 A comparison Oscar Wilde: *The Importance of Being Earnest* Trevor Griffiths: *Comedians*	50
7 Novelisation Wole Soyinka: *Camwood on the Leaves*	53
8 Programme notes Tom Stoppard: *Jumpers*	55

Three	**Poems**	**59**

    What is a poem?   59
    What do we look for in a poem?   63
    How might one write about a poem?   67

        1   Poetry and politics   R. S. Thomas: *Selected Poems*   67
        2   Poetry in time   Robin Skelton (ed.): *Poetry of the Thirties*   69
        3   Poetry in place   Derek Walcott: *Selected Poetry*   72
        4   Thoughts on a second reading   Philip Larkin: *The Whitsun Weddings*   75
        5   Poetry out loud   George MacBeth (ed.): *Poetry 1900 to 1975*   77
        6   Abridgement   William Wordsworth: *The Prelude*   79
        7   Art and life   William Blake: *Songs of Innocence and Experience*   81
        8   An obituary   Rupert Brooke, Wilfred Owen, Isaac Rosenberg – Brian Gardner (ed.): *Up the Line to Death*   84

Four	**Non-fiction**	**87**

    What is non-fiction?   87
    What do we look for in non-fiction?   91
    How might one write about non-fiction?   94

        1   Travel writing   Laurie Lee: *As I Walked Out One Midsummer Morning* D. H. Lawrence: *Sea and Sardinia*   94
        2   Author bias   Lytton Strachey: *Eminent Victorians*   97
        3   The selective memory   Graham Greene: *A Sort of Life*   99
        4   Interview with the author   Flora Thompson: *Lark Rise to Candleford*   102
        5   Publisher's blurb   Maya Angelou: *I Know Why the Caged Bird Sings*   104
        6   A participant's journal   Antony Sher: *Year of the King*   107
        7   Debate   Virginia Woolf: *A Room of One's Own*   110
        8   A personal view   Bob Dixon: *Catching them Young*   113

Five	**The 'long' coursework essay**	**116**

    What are the requirements?   116
    What line might one take?   118
    How might one write the essay?   124

        'The Angry Young Man':   John Wain: *Hurry on Down* Kingsley Amis: *Lucky Jim*   John Osborne: *Look Back in Anger*   124

    Final thoughts   132

Index   **133**

PREFACE

Coursework is now an element of many 'alternative' English Literature syllabuses at A and AS level. The AEB's Syllabuses 660 and 986, the London Board's Syllabus 170 (Paper 4C) and the JMB's A Level Syllabus C are only some of the best known. More and more teachers are opting for coursework syllabuses, and candidate numbers are rising in proportion.

It always was a forlorn hope that A Level students would, in two years, learn to be literary critics. Criticism calls for (implicit if not explicit) comparison, and no student at 18+ has read enough to make comparisons that are more discernment than feeling. It is right, therefore, that we should harness feeling.

Coursework syllabuses have proved to be the decisive factor in a revaluation of what it means to 'do' English Literature at an advanced level. A Chief Examiner will now look for 'variety and innovation', even 'adventure', in approaches to literature, and the sound of 'the candidate's own voice' will be welcome in place of the plots and quotes orthodoxy of the past. The 'genuinely individual engagement' with chosen texts that is wanted cannot be imposed – it cannot even be taught. John Gross has ridiculed the idea that Literature can be thought of as a *discipline*:

> Literature can be strenuous or difficult or deeply disturbing; it can be a hundred things – but a discipline is not one of them.
>
> *The Rise and Fall of the Man of Letters*, Penguin Books

The above-quoted Chief Examiner, in reference to views about the relationship between Aston and Mick in Pinter's *The Caretaker*, went so far as to say that: 'the more alternatives (candidates) had considered, and the more unsure they were, the more marks they gained'. That is why this book is called *Alternative English*.

Teachers exchange innovative ideas at consortium meetings, and to teachers who attend such meetings, there will be little in this book that is new. Students do not attend such meetings, however, and they may not be as open to ideas exchanged in class as we may like to think. Mass-produced revision notes are testimony to their need of extra-curricular support in the past. These will be superseded as the examinations that spawned them are superseded by open-book papers and coursework that calls for engagement of a 'post-critical' sort.

But students will still need support. This book seeks to offer suggestions for experiment in various ways of responding to various examples of writing. (Scottish and European writing may be considered to be under-represented among these examples. It is open to the teacher to substitute such writing for any of the texts used here by way of illustration.) They are suggestions of the kind that innovative teachers might make.

It is hoped that *Alternative English* will thus be a book that teachers will feel able to commend to students in the context of 'supported self-study'. It may suggest teaching strategies, but the book's primary aim is to stimulate the student's own thinking, reading and writing. The 'you' therefore to whom the book is addressed is the student.

C. Swatridge

ACKNOWLEDGEMENTS

The author would like to record his thanks to, and respect for, his colleagues in the English Department at Reigate College.

The author and publishers wish to thank the following who have kindly given permission for the use of copyright material:

Bryan Appleyard for extract from *The Times*, 16.10.86, p. 102 • The Associated Examining Board for extracts from their A Level English Syllabus (660), pp. 116, 118 • Michael Billington for a review of *Volpone*, the *Guardian*, 1983, p. 46 • Jonathan Cape Ltd. for an extract from *Chips With Everything* by Arnold Wesker, pp. 33–4 • Michael Codron Ltd. for an advertisement of Tom Stoppard's *Jumpers* at the Aldwych Theatre, p. 56 • the *Daily Telegraph* for an extract from a review of E. L. Doctorow's *World's Fair*, p. 1 • Faber and Faber Ltd. for 'Days' and 'Ignorance' from *The Whitsun Weddings* by Philip Larkin, pp. 76–7; short extracts from *Endgame* by Samuel Beckett, p. 32; *Translations* by Brian Friel, p. 35; 'An Eclogue for Christmas' from *The Collected Poems of Louis MacNeice*, p. 71; 'The Cave of Making' from *Collected Poems* by W. H. Auden, p. 67; Nobel Lecture 1983 from *A Moving Target* by William Golding, p. 5; Part I of *Murder in the Cathedral* by T. S. Eliot, p. 30; *Comedians* by Trevor Griffiths pp. 52–3; *Jumpers* by Tom Stoppard, pp. 57–8; and 'The Estranging Sea', 'The Castaway' and 'Dark August' from *Collected Poems 1948–84* by Derek Walcott, pp. 73–4 • the *Guardian* for extracts from various issues of the *Guardian* • Jeffrey Gillie for a letter published in the *Guardian*, p. 60 • Grafton Books for extracts from 'Affinity' and 'A Welsh Testament' by R. S. Thomas, p. 68 • Heinemann Educational Books Ltd., for material from the back cover of the paperback version of *A Man for all Seasons* by Robert Bolt, p. 29 • David Higham Associates Ltd. on behalf of the Estate of the author for material from *Under Milk Wood* by Dylan Thomas, Dent, pp. 48–9; and 'I have longed to move away' from *Quite Early One Morning* by Dylan Thomas, pp. 70–1 • Park Honan for extracts from 'Problems of Literary Biography', *Words International*, Vol. 1, No. 3, pp. 89–90 • Michael Howlett for a letter published in the *Guardian*, p. 60 • the *Independent* for extracts from the 10.6.88 and 18.10.88 issues of the *Independent*, pp. 78–9, 123 • Roland John for a review, *South East Arts Review*, Issue 20, p. 93 • *London Magazine* for extracts from a review by John Figueroa, *London Magazine*, Vol. 21, April/May, 1981, pp. 73, 74 • Rhona Martin for a review, *South East Arts Review*, Issue 19, p. 92 • Methuen, London for an extract from 'Camwood on the Leaves' from *Six Plays* by Wole Soyinka, pp. 54–5; and an extract from *The Caretaker* by Harold Pinter, pp. 38–9 • Stephen Meyer for a letter published in the *Guardian*, p. 60 • Midland Examining Group for an extract from *Guidelines for Teachers on Advanced Level English Paper 9000/10* • David R. Morgan for 'That's Rich' by Paul Daly from 'Fairfield' by David R. Morgan, *Words International*, February 1988, p. 66 • John Murray, Publishers, Ltd. for 'The Last Laugh' and an extract from 'Executive' from *Collected Poems* by John Betjeman, pp. 61, 67 • *New Statesman* for John Coleman's review of *Nineteen Eighty-Four* by George Orwell, *New Statesman*, 12.10.84, p. 25 • the *New York Review of Books* for material from a review of E. L. Doctorow's *World's Fair*,

© 1985, Nyrev, Inc., p. 1 • the *Observer* for an extract by Angela Carter on *The Great Gatsby* by F. Scott Fitzgerald, *Observer Magazine*, 24.2.80, pp. 25–6 • Michael Paffard for an extract from a letter published in the *Guardian*, p. 62 • Penguin Books Ltd. for a biographical sketch of Virginia Woolf on the back of the Penguin issue of *A Room of One's Own*, p. 111; and an extract from the back cover of *Lark Rise to Candleford*, © cover text Penguin Books, 1973, p. 104 • *Radio Times* for material from various issues of the *Radio Times*, pp. 4, 11, 16, 17, 36, 94, 119, 120, 121, 122 • Tessa Sayle Agency on behalf of the authors for an extract from *Oh What a Lovely War* by Joan Littlewood's Theatre Workshop, Charles Chilton and members of the original cast, Methuen, © 1965 by Joan Littlewood's Theatre Productions Ltd., p. 31 • Mrs M. Scarfe for 'Beauty, Boloney' by Francis Scarfe from *Poetry of the Thirties*, edited Robin Skelton, Penguin Books, p. 71 • Antony Sher for extract from *Year of the King*, Chatto and Windus, pp. 108–9 • Keith Spence for a review, *South East Arts Review*, Issue 17, p. 92 • Sutton Amateur Dramatic Club for a handbill by Michael Coghlan, p. 41 • Times Newspapers Ltd. for articles and extracts from 'Twin Odysseys' by Jill Burrows, *TES*, 28.10.83, p. 45; 'Well Said' by Ann FitzGerald, *TES*, 10.83, p. 45; 'Way Back When?' by Michael Church, *TES*, 10.83, p. 46; review by Jill Burrows of *Measure for Measure*, *TES*, 28.10.83, p. 42; the obituary of W. H. Auden, *TT*, 1.10.73, p. 65; summaries of *Nice Work* and *The Lost Father*, *TES*, 21.10.88, p. 87; Lifeline article by Iola Smith, *TES*, 24.10.86, p. 20; and the headline 'Teachers blamed for making English dull', p. ix • The Young Vic for biographical information of actors in their 1987 production of *Comedians* by Trevor Griffiths, p. 52

We are also grateful to the following for permission to reproduce photographs and artwork:

BBC Enterprises Ltd., p. 12 • Jonathan Cape Ltd. for drawing of Little Chandler from Granada edition of *Dubliners*, p. 22 • Chatto and Windus for dust cover of *The Lost Father*, p. 87 (right) • © Cockerell, Cambridge for marbled paper used on the cover • Michael Daley for illustration used on front cover • Andre Deutsch Ltd. for dust cover of *As I Walked Out One Midsummer Morning*, p. 95 • Faber and Faber Ltd., p. 78 (below) • Mark Gerson, p. 122 • © Fay Godwin, p. 76 • Heinemann International (photograph © George Hallet), p. 27 • the *Independent*, p. 105 • Douglas Jeffery, p. 46 • National Portrait Gallery, pp. 85, 111 • Bert Parnaby/The Young Vic (photograph by Jan Harvey), p. 52 (left) • Courtesy of Pathé Releasing (photograph supplied by British Film Institute), p. 17 • Scope Features, pp. 4, 63 • Martin Secker and Warburg Ltd. for dust cover of *Nice Work*, p. 87 (left), and photograph and dust cover of *White Boy Running*, p. 121 • © Antony Sher, for drawing from *Year Of The King*, Chatto and Windus, p. 109 • David Smith (cartoon appeared in the *Guardian*), p. 107 • *South East Arts Review*, p. 92 • Times Newspapers Ltd., p. 65 • Virgin Vision (photograph supplied by British Film Institute), p. 24 • Welsh Arts Council, p. 68 • Colin Wheeler (cartoon appeared in the *Independent* on 19 June 1988), p. 78 (above) • Richard Willson/*The Times*, 1986, p. 100 • The Young Vic, p. 52 (right)

Every effort has been made to trace all the copyright holders, and we apologise if any have been overlooked.

INTRODUCTION

Her Majesty's Inspectors (HMI) carried out a survey of the teaching of A Level English Literature. Their findings were published in 1987. Courses in this subject had changed little in 30 years, they said. There was still the old narrow concentration on essay and context questions, and lessons were still dominated by the requirements of examinations.

These headlines appeared in newspapers on the day following publication of the HMI Report:

Teachers blamed for making English dull
By John Clare, Education Correspondent

The Times, 1987

Literature at A level 'lifeless'
By Sarah Boseley, Education Correspondent

The Guardian, 1987

Examinations of an unreformed sort have had a baneful influence on the teaching and learning of English Literature at A Level; there is no doubt about that. But open-book examinations and coursework syllabuses are agents of change for the better. The coursework element ranges from 30 per cent in the JMB's A Level Syllabus C to 60 per cent in the AEB's AS Level Syllabus 986.

Coursework has proved to be more than just a fairer means of assessing what students 'can do'; it has raised fundamental questions about what we should be doing when we 'do' literature at this level. Teachers can no longer blame the examiners for holding back progress. As the syllabuses have changed, so have the examiners and what they are looking for. If they have looked for standard answers to standard questions in the past, they are looking for feeling responses and individuality now.

They want you, the student, to *engage with* texts. What do they mean by this? They mean that they want you to explore ways of entering into dialogue with authors, exchanging ideas with them, as it were, joining with them in the creative process, and responding to their visions and the ways in which they have expressed them with contrary or complementary visions of your own. There is no one right way in which to interpret a play or novel or poem. There is not even a best way. There are, simply, sensitive and insensitive ways of reading a work. The more open and unprejudiced your approach to it, the more you attempt to relate what you read to your own experience, the more your interpretation will admit of alternatives, and *the more you read*, the more sensitive is your reading of any one work likely to be.

What the examiners want is that you should study the texts set or chosen. What they quite specifically do *not* want is that you should retail the views of established critics; and still less that you should parrot the interpretations (or the language) of the writers of revision notes or crib-books. Where this book may seem to make judgements, these are offered as stimuli to your own thinking, not as statements ready-made for quotation.

It is the intention of this book, above all, to be suggestive. It is not a textbook: it is more in the nature of a handbook, to be dipped into for ideas. And where it is suggested that you write a programme note for Stoppard's *Jumpers,* or that you interview Flora Thompson, author of *Lark Rise,* it is always for you to decide whether to write the programme note for a dramatisation of the latter, or to interview Tom Stoppard. (Almost) every suggestion that is made for writing on one text is one that you could apply in quite another context. What is important is that it should be *your* decision, made for reasons that *you* can explain. The success (or otherwise) of this book will be measured by the extent to which it helps you to draw upon your own vocabulary, to respond to what you read on your own account.

ONE

Novels and short stories

What is a novel?

One might as well ask: how long is a piece of string? The term has been stretched so far that it would be more appropriate to speak of elastic than string. When the novel is not 'dead', it is alive in a hundred and one forms. But the first requirement of a novel would seem to be that it be *fiction*.

> ***World's Fair* by E. L. Doctorow**
>
> Social historians are going to be grateful to E. L. Doctorow. *World's Fair* is a wonderful time machine, sweeping the reader into that world of movie serials – Dick Tracey, Flash Gordon, Zorro – of amateur jazz bands, of phonographs, the Hindenburg, the World's Fair itself.
>
> *Sunday Telegraph*

> *World's Fair* is authoritatively documented and evocative... to it Doctorow brings so much observed period detail that a reader who has lived through the Thirties will experience repeated tremors, if not shocks, of recognition.
>
> *New York Review of Books* (from the rear cover of the Picador edition 1985)

Can what looks like autobiography be fiction? *World's Fair* won the 1986 American Book Award for Fiction, and the *Daily Telegraph* called it: 'A moving and beautiful novel.' So perhaps we have to accept that it is a novel. What can certainly be said is that it is a work of the imagination.

A second requirement would seem to be that it be in *prose*.

In June 1986, Robert Nye reviewed two new novels in the *Guardian*. One was *Persephone* by Jenny Joseph (Bloodaxe Books). He said of it:

> Jenny Joseph's *Persephone* is just the sort of book that never gets reviewed. Called a new kind of novel by its publisher, though not by its author, it mixes prose and verse in about equal measure... As Jenny Joseph reminds us in a note at the end, mixing verse and prose is in fact an old practice (...) What is unusual about Joseph's book is that the story line goes through the verse, with the prose bits as a sort of light relief (...)
>
> *The Guardian*, 1986

The other was *The Golden Gate* by Vikram Seth (Faber):

> *The Golden Gate* is a story of a group of young and not-so-young Californian yuppies living in the glittering shadows of the Golden Gate Bridge (...) Vikram Seth's extravaganza is great, it makes frenetic fun, and I would hate to put anyone off by revealing that he has chosen to couch the whole thing in a sort of sonnet sequence (...) Yes, this is novels-in-verse week, and why not?
>
> *The Guardian*, 1986

Why not, indeed? 'When it is poetry' is no longer the answer to the question: 'When is a novel not a novel?'

A third requirement, surely, is that there be a *plot*, or story-line. A novel without a story would seem to be the equivalent of a journal without events, an essay without an argument, a rhapsody without a tune.

Philip Howard reviewed *The Rat* by Gunter Grass in *The Times* in June 1987. He said that if we take a novel to be a plot, with characters whom we know by their actions, and a story that has a beginning, middle, and end, then *The Rat* is not a novel.

It would seem, then, that the novel does not have to have a story to be a novel. There have been novels that have been bundles of letters and entries in a diary. There have been novels without characters, and there have been novels without punctuation. (Perhaps what we lack is an alternative name. We call a work like Samuel Beckett's *The Unnameable* a 'novel' because it is the only word we have for a lengthy piece of prose non-fiction.) All that a novel needs for it to *be* a novel is for a novelist, publisher or reviewer to say: this is a novel. Can you suggest an alternative name?

What is a short story?

If a novel does not have to have a story, does a short story have to have a story?

We might define a story as: an account of people making things happen, or of things happening to people. Can you suggest an alternative definition?

Nothing 'happens' in Mel Calman's short story 'The Fifty Minute Hour' (*Penguin Modern Stories 9*, 1971): a man sits, waiting for an appointment with his psychiatrist thinking about life and death. Nothing happens; he just thinks. 'Think' is not a doing word.

But if 'The Fifty Minute Hour' is not a short story, it is nothing. It is *a slice of life* – and this is what many short stories are.

Mel Calman's slice of life is short, there is no doubt about that. It runs to about 500 words, which makes it very short.

And this we can say about the short story with most certainty: it must be short. A long short story is a *novella* (like *The Turn of The Screw* by Henry James, or *The Fox* by D. H. Lawrence). And, of course, a long novella is a novel. We leave it to publishers to decide where to draw the line.

Note
In what follows, what is said about the novel applies equally to the short story – or the collection of short stories – and to the novella.

What do we look for in a novel?

The novel that does not have a story and that is not about people is the exception that proves the rule. Let us be concerned here with the rule and not with the exception.

A story can only have one merit according to E. M. Forster, that of making the reader want to know what happens next. Conversely, it can only have one fault, that of making the reader *not* want to know what happens next.

A story is a succession of events, arranged, as Forster says, 'in their time sequence'. Event A happened . . . and then B . . . and then C, and then . . . and so on, until what William Golding calls 'a satisfactory end-point' is reached. To the extent that a novel makes a reader want to move eagerly from Event A to Event B, and from Event B to Event C, and so on, until Event Z, it has a good chance of surviving. It has a good chance, that is, of being published, of being reviewed, of being bought, of being

Alternative English

borrowed, of being reprinted, and – accolade of accolades – of being chosen as a set book. To the extent that the novel does not make the reader want to know what happens next, its chances of being published, and of its being *well* reviewed, are small.

In this sense, the novel is no different from any one of half a dozen television soap operas.

12.00 News
Weather followed by
Dallas
If at First You Don't...
The killer prepares to strike again.
Written by DAVID PAULSEN
Directed by LEONARD KATZMAN (R)
★ CEEFAX SUBTITLES

12.05pm Neighbours
Clive gives a verdict on Dan's health. Charlene and Kelly put Mike and Scott in an embarrassing situation.
Written by CHRIS MCCOURT
(For cast see page 73. Shown again at 5.35pm)

3.30pm Sons and Daughters
Alison is shattered when David says he never wants her back. Charlie is torn between lovers and old friends. Wayne and Mary are feeling strange about being in such close proximity after learning they are half-brother and sister.
For cast, see Wednesday

2.00pm EastEnders
by JANE HOLLOWOOD and TONY MCHALE
'Angie's gone for good, Sharon. There's no way she's ever coming back to Walford.'
Series producer JULIA SMITH
★ CEEFAX SUBTITLES

8.00pm Brookside
The first of this week's visits to the Merseyside housing estate. Will Penny bring Franco's books to Sizzler? Growler has his problems — but what's wrong with Sammy?
Oracle subtitles page 888

Billy	John McArdle
Harry	Bill Dean
Ralph	Ray Dunbobbin
Sheila	Sue Johnston
Chrissy	Eithne Browne
Growler	Kevin Carson
Sammy	Rachael Lindsay
Barry	Paul Usher
Bumper	James Mawdsley
Kathy	Noreen Kershaw
Franco	Vincenzo Nicoli
Penny	Lynda Rooke
Sizzler	Renny Krupinski

WRITER ANDY LYNCH
DESIGNER CAROL SHEERAN
DIRECTOR TIM FYWELL
EXECUTIVE PRODUCER PHIL REDMOND

Mersey Television Production

8.15–9.00 Dynasty
starring
John Forsythe as Blake
Linda Evans as Krystle
Joan Collins as Alexis
Gordon Thompson as Adam
Jack Coleman as Steven
Michael Nader as Dex
Emma Samms as Fallon
Heather Locklear as Sammy Jo
John James as Jeff
Terri Garber as Leslie

James Healey as Sean
Leann Hunley as Dana
The Scandal
'If I go down, I take everyone with me!' As the truth about Sean begins to spill out, Blake flies to Africa to get more proof – but it's a trip that threatens his reputation and his life.
Karen........STEPHANIE DUNNAM
Jesse......CHRISTOPHER ALLPORT
Neal McVane.....PAUL BURKE
Thresher............DANIEL DAVIS
Written by FRANK V. FURINO
Directed by IRVING J. MOORE
★ CEEFAX SUBTITLES

7.30pm Coronation Street
Ken is determined to get *The Recorder* out on time, but Deirdre is anxious there might be madness in his method. And Sandra Stubbs agrees to meet her estranged husband.
See page 10
Oracle subtitles page 888

Vera Duckworth	Elizabeth Dawn
Jack Duckworth	William Tarmey
Deirdre	Anne Kirkbride
Ken Barlow	William Roache
Bet Gilroy	Julie Goodyear
Betty Turpin	Betty Driver
Gloria Todd	Sue Jenkins
Sandra Stubbs	Sally Watts
Fiona Cavanagh	Sharon Muircroft
Percy Sugden	Bill Waddington
Alf Roberts	Bryan Mosley
Mavis Riley	Thelma Barlow
Sally Webster	Sally Whittaker
Kevin Webster	Michael Le Vell
Gail Tilsley	Helen Worth
Ronnie Stubbs	Eamon Boland
Jason Stubbs	Paul Simpson
Mike Baldwin	Johnny Briggs
Alan Bradley	Mark Eden
Audrey Roberts	Sue Nicholls
Emily Bishop	Eileen Derbyshire
Bob Stratham	Michael Goldie

WRITER STEPHEN MALLATRATT
STORIES TOM ELLIOTT, JANE WOODROW
DIRECTOR NICHOLAS FERGUSON
DESIGNER ANN SWARBRICK
PRODUCER BILL PODMORE

Granada Television Production

Radio Times and *TV Times*, 1988

These have a story (a succession of events leading – repeatedly – to a satisfactory, interim end-point) and they have people. And, to judge by the viewing figures, millions (and millions, and millions) of viewers want to know what happens next.

Indeed, if the novel was all story and nothing else, it is difficult to see how it could compete with the soap opera. What the novel can do, that the soap opera *cannot* do, is get right inside the minds of the actors. The viewer can watch Sharon and Clive and Sue Ellen and Charlie, draw conclusions about what sort of people they are and love them or hate them; but he or she cannot really enter their lives in an imaginative, sensitive and enriching way.

William Golding (in the speech of acceptance of his Nobel Prize for Literature) said of the novel:

> There is no other medium in which we can live for so long and so intimately with a character. That is the service a novel renders. It performs no less an act than the rescue and the preservation of the individuality and dignity of the single being, be it man, woman, or child. No other art, I claim, can so thread in and out of a single mind and body, so live another life. It does ensure that at the very least a human being shall be seen to be more than just one billionth of one billion.

But if David Paulsen made a book of 'Dallas' (he must forgive me if he has, in fact, done so and I have not noticed), if Chris McCourt made a book of 'Neighbours' and Andy Lynch did likewise of 'Brookside', would these books be novels? Is there still something more to a novel than a novelisation?

A novel that is going to survive, and be set for study, must do one or both of the following:

1   It must say something original about *life*, not just for its own time, but for all time. It must be, to some extent, prophetic, not in the sense that it looks forward, but in the sense that it warns, or that it brings something of importance to the attention of its readers.

    Franz Kafka in *The Trial* (1925) described state bureaucracy and legalism at their most nightmarish. His hero was the innocent victim of anonymous men working by devious means to unknown ends.

    As Kafka gave his name to bureaucracy gone mad, so George Orwell gave his name to dictatorship bent on power for its own sake. *Nineteen Eighty-Four* is still a powerful warning (*not* a prophecy) for all that 1984 is way behind us.

    Jane Austen's *Emma*, George Eliot's *Mill on the Floss*, and Lawrence's *The Rainbow* have been set texts for years past. They stand in what the critic F. R. Leavis called the 'Great Tradition'. Books that have 'set appeal' today may include Alice Walker's *The Color Purple,* and Nadine Gordimer's *Six Feet of the Country*.

These latter works are less dramatic warnings, and neither is, perhaps, likely to be called 'great'. But they are both sensitive, insightful, humane accounts of the black experience in America and South Africa respectively. There was art in their making: there is structure, there is characterisation, and there is a figurative use of language there.

2. It must, in some way, advance the art of the novel. John Fowles' *The French Lieutenant's Woman* does not warn its readers; it does not draw anything of importance about life to their attention. As the writer of the blurb on the back of the Panther edition (1971) put it, the novel evokes 'in perfect detail the Victorian world of repressed sexuality and cruel hypocrisy'. This might have been enough to guarantee that the novel would be a 'bestseller' (and the film version probably helped). There is no question but that the reader wants to know what happens next.

> *The French Lieutenant's Woman* is a wonder of contemporary fiction ... you never want it to end.
>
> Life Magazine

> A splendid, lucid, profoundly satisfying work of art, a book which I want almost immediately to read again.
>
> New Statesman

That the novel is 'a work of art' might have earned it a place on a list of set books, but what guaranteed its place is the fact that it enlarged the art of the novel, and so made the novel a more potent medium.

In Chapter 13, John Fowles breaks off from his account of the thinkings and doings of Charles Smithson, Sarah Woodruff and Mrs Poulteney, and addresses the reader directly.

Thirteen

> For the drift of the Maker is dark, an Isis hid by the veil ...
> TENNYSON, Maud (1855)

I do not know. This story I am telling is all imagination. These characters I create never existed outside my own mind. If I have pretended until now to know my characters' minds and innermost thoughts, it is because I am writing in (just as I have assumed some of the vocabulary and 'voice' of) a convention universally accepted at the time of my story: that the novelist stands next to God. He may not know all, yet he tries to pretend that he does. But I live in the age of Alain Robbe-Grillet and Roland Barthes; if this is a novel, it cannot be a novel in the modern sense of the word (...)

The novelist is still a god, since he creates (and not even the most aleatory avant-garde modern novel has managed to extirpate its author completely); what has changed is that we are no longer the gods of the Victorian image, omniscient and decreeing; but in the new theological image, with freedom our first principle, not authority.

I have disgracefully broken the illusion? No. My characters still exist, and in a reality no less, or no more, real than the one I have just broken. Fiction is woven into all, as a Greek observed some two and a half thousand years ago. I find this new reality (or unreality) more valid; and I would have you share my own sense that I do not fully control these creatures of my mind, any more than you control (...) your children, colleagues, friends or even yourself.

Granada edition, pp. 85, 86–7

Who are Alain Robbe-Grillet and Roland Barthes? Robbe-Grillet was a leading exponent of the French *nouveau roman*, or anti-novel, of the 1950s. He makes no comment on the psychology or ideology of his characters. They are, and they do, and there's an end of it. It is for the reader to judge them if he or she will – it is not for the novelist to do this.

Barthes – another Frenchman – was a critic who refused to believe that it was his business to analyse the meaning of a work or to assess its value. Rather, that is, he claimed no more right than any reader has to decide what a novel means. Every reader, he said, brings meanings of his or her own to a novel (or poem, or play) because they bring their own experiences to it. Hence John Fowles' unwillingness to assume ultimate control of his characters. None of us is God; everyone who reads, and believes (or who suspends disbelief), is a priest.

And this point brings us back to our Introduction. It is for you, the reader, to decide what a novel is 'about'. You do not have to be a critic – a god – to do this. You must simply be prepared to *engage with* the text, sympathetically, and consider alternative interpretations – the more the better; the more divergent, the more adventurous, the more existential, the better. The following pages contain suggestions as to how you might do this.

Note

The Examination Boards are happy that candidates should be 'creative': that is that they should write imaginary letters, and journals, and adaptations (the dramatisation of a short story, for instance); but it is stressed that no more than a minority of coursework pieces should be of this kind. Where candidates do write creative pieces, they should justify the style and content of the writing by reference to the original. A variety of approaches to reading and response *is* wanted, but in all the writing that they do, candidates should aim to demonstrate their knowledge and understanding of the text. This is primary. Beyond this requirement, the most highly regarded pieces of work will be those that show a 'genuinely individual engagement' with the chosen text.

How might one write about a novel?

1 Another point of view

Sometimes an author creates characters, and then, like God, stands apart from them. The author/creator is, as it were, a dispassionate observer of events – a reporter, or recording angel.

There may be a main character through whose eyes we see all that goes on, and through whose musings we understand it. It is often the case that we are intended to sympathise with this hero/heroine, and more often than not, the author introduces us to this character before all others, because we tend to see things through the eyes of the first person we meet.

Sometimes, again, the author takes the part of one of the characters in the novel – perhaps the main character, and perhaps not. Instead of using the third person (he or she), the author writes as I – the first person. (The author may refer to the reader in the second person – you – as John Fowles does in Chapter 13 of *The French Lieutenant's Woman*. But this is unusual in the modern novel.)

L. P. Hartley's *The Go-Between* begins (famously) with these words:

PROLOGUE

The past is a foreign country: they do things differently there.

When I came upon the diary it was lying at the bottom of a rather battered red cardboard collar box, in which as a small boy I kept my Eton collars. Someone, probably my mother, had filled it with treasures dating from those days.

Penguin edition, p. 7

The author takes the part of a twelve/thirteen-year-old boy, Leo Colston, on holiday at Brandham Hall, Norfolk. We meet him at the beginning of Chapter 1 on the threshold of his holiday, his adolescence, and the action of the novel:

CHAPTER 1

The eighth of July was a Sunday and on the following Monday I left West Hatch, the village where we lived near Salisbury, for Brandham Hall. My mother arranged that my Aunt Charlotte, a Londoner, should take me across London. Between bouts of stomach-turning trepidation I looked forward wildly to the visit.

(p. 22)

A school friend, Marcus Maudsley, has invited Leo to spend July with him. His older sister, Marian, is betrothed to Hugh, Lord Trimingham, to whom the family pays rent. Clearly the marriage would be convenient. But Marian is secretly in love with Ted Burgess, a rough-cut local farmer. Leo finds himself acting as the message-bearer between the Virgin and Aquarius, the Water-Carrier.

We see all the action, from beginning to end, through Leo's young, innocent, expectant eyes. What we learn, we learn at *his* speed, and what we understand is filtered through *his* understanding. The novel is thus not about 'the adult world of passion, deception and hypocrisy' (to quote the rear-cover blurb), it is about 'a young boy's traumatic initiation' into this world – which is a very different thing.

Hartley might have written the novel from the point of view of its tragic hero, Ted Burgess; or from that of its heroine, and *femme fatale*, Marian Maudsley. The novel is 'about' the unconventional love-affair between these two, and Leo's mercurial part in it.

We learn a lot about both Ted and Marian. We are given strong physical impressions of them:

[Marian] *. . . she was tall, even by grown-up standards (. . .) Her father's long eyelids dropped over her eyes, leaving under them a glint of blue so deep and liquid that it might have been shining through an unshed tear. Her hair was bright with sunshine, but her face, which was full like her mother's, only pale rose-pink instead of cream, wore a stern brooding look that her small curved nose made almost hawk-like.*

(p. 37)

[Ted] *. . . he stretched both arms high above his chest, which was so white it might have belonged to another person, except below his neck where the sun had burnt a* *copper breastplate (. . .) He pulled his shirt over his head, and his corduroy trousers over his wet bathing-slip; stuffed his feet into thick grey socks, and pulled his boots on.*

(p. 57)

We learn much about the personality of each. Both can be gentle with Leo, and formidable, by turns. Both are emotional, moody, changeable people. We conspire with them, and wish their passion well. Marian is aware that she has made an impression on Leo. She speaks to him about Ted:

> *'We sometimes write each other notes . . . on business matters. And you say you like taking them.'*
> *'Oh yes, I do,' I said, enthusiastically.*
> *'Because you like T – Mr Burgess?'*
> *I knew she wanted me to say I did, and I was ready to accommodate her, the more so that an overwhelming desire to testify came over me, and I saw my chance to voice it.*
> *'Yes, but there's another reason.'*
> *'What is it?'*
> *I had no idea that when I came to them the words would be so difficult to say, but at last I brought them out.*
> *'Because I like you.'*

(pp. 99–100)

On the whole the reader likes Marian also. And it is altogether more likely that the reader will like Ted than dislike him, for all that 'he's rather rough'.

Chapters 11 and 12 are in many ways the pivotal chapters of the novel. All the main characters take part in what, in the context of the novel, is rather more than a simple cricket match.

 You could interpret the cricket-match scene from the point of view of either Marian or Ted Burgess. You would need:

1 to explain the significance of this match in the context of the novel as a whole, and
2 to explain your interpretation of Marian's/Ted's feelings by reference to other events and situations in the novel.

Alternatively, you could 'see' another significant scene through the eyes of Trimingham, Mrs Maudsley, or Marcus. There is information enough about each of these characters. How might Trimingham view the events of Chapter 8, for instance? Or Marcus, the supper at the village hall, in Chapter 13?

2 A letter from one character to another

A novelist will very often embed a letter in the third- or first-person narrative. There is no surer way of conveying a character's feelings on a subject (and perhaps of imparting useful information to the reader also) than to give vent to them in a letter. Hartley (in *The Go-Between*) has Leo write to his mother in Chapter 16; and Mrs Colston's reply is given in full in Chapter 20 ('P.S. What a long letter! But I thought you would like to know *exactly* how I felt.')

Whole chapters of Alice Walker's *The Color Purple* are given over to letters from Nettie to her sister. And whole novels have been in letter (or epistolary) form. Samuel Richardson's *Pamela* is only the best known epistolary novel because it was the first of many. William Golding's *Rites of Passage* is a letter of a sort from a voyager to his 'Honoured Godfather'.

It is odd, perhaps, that there are no letters in Jane Austen's *Northanger Abbey*. Maggie Wadey dramatised the novel for BBC2, and the novelist Fay Weldon said this of the film:

A teenager in love

That's Jane Austen's heroine Catherine Morland, who yearns for romance and adventure – and finds it, Southfork style – at Northanger Abbey. Today she'd be a 'Dallas' fan, writes Fay Weldon

Maggie Wadey's dramatisation turns out to be a classic of a classic. A single concentrated film, as suits this short, animated, animating novel; not just lovely to look at but witty, lively, romantic and wonderfully endearing. It's the story of a girl, her head filled with the *Dallas/Dynasty* of her time (the popular Novel of Terror and Sentiment, as it was known then; gothic bodice-ripper to us), who nearly ruins her own chances of true love because of her fantasies. What is fact, what is fiction, when love itself is such a fictional, unlikely event? The notion preoccupied the young Jane Austen, as it has writers ever since, and her fictionalised essay on the theme, written with a kind of light, joyous concentration, was *Northanger Abbey*. And the spell is as strong now as ever.

No need then to approach BBC2's version with that nervous dread most of us reserve for the culturally respectable – it was a lightweight book to begin with, not serious like *Persuasion*. Purists will not be happy at a scene missing here, a scene added there, but there is such wit, and fun, and pace, and plot and speculation – not to mention worldly wisdom – it is impossible not simply to rejoice.

Radio Times

Just as Leo Colston was on the threshold of adolescence and Brandham Hall, Norfolk, at the beginning of *The Go-Between*, so Catherine Morland is on the threshold of young womanhood and her début in Bath, at the beginning of *Northanger Abbey*. The novel is a burlesque of the conventional, romantic, sentimental 'gothic' novel of Jane Austen's time. It is made plain, therefore, that Catherine Morland is *not* the conventional heroine of such a novel. Before she left home, her sister, 'intimate friend and confidante', Sally Morland:

> *... neither insisted on Catherine's writing by every post, nor exacted her promise of transmitting the character of every new acquaintance, nor a detail of every interesting conversation that Bath might provide.*

Penguin edition, p. 42

Katherine Schlesinger as Catherine Morland in the BBC production of *Northanger Abbey* 1987

Henry Tilney is a 'gentlemanlike young man', twenty-four or twenty-five years old. He is 'rather tall', and has 'a very intelligent and lively eye'. This is the young man with whom Catherine Morland has the good sense to fall in love. Early in the novel, however, he puts his intelligence to use by teasing the young and naïve Catherine:

> *'I see what you think of me,' said he gravely – 'I shall make but a poor figure in your journal tomorrow.'*
> *'My journal!'*

> 'Yes, I know exactly what you will say: Friday, went to the Lower Rooms, wore my sprigged muslin robe with blue trimmings – plain black shoes – appeared to much advantage; but was strangely harassed by a queer, half-witted man, who would make me dance with him, and distressed me by his nonsense' (. . .)
>
> 'But, perhaps, I keep no journal.'
>
> 'Perhaps you are not sitting in this room, and I am not sitting by you. These are points in which a doubt is equally possible. Not keep a journal! (. . .) Everybody allows that the talent of writing agreeable letters is peculiarly female. Nature may have done something, but I am sure it must be essentially assisted by the practice of keeping a journal.'
>
> 'I have sometimes thought,' said Catherine, doubtingly, 'whether ladies do write so much better letters than gentlemen! That is – I should not think the superiority was always on our side.'
>
> 'As far as I have had opportunity of judging, it appears to me that the usual style of letter-writing among women is faultless, except in three particulars.'
>
> 'And what are they?'
>
> 'A general deficiency of subject, a total inattention to stops, and a very frequent ignorance of grammar.'
>
> (pp. 48–9)

We are told *about* letters in the novel: Catherine refers to a letter received by 'a particular friend of mine', from London, in which a preview is given of a forthcoming novel of a sort 'very shocking indeed' (p. 126). Much play is made of the impending, and actual receipt of a letter from James Morland, Catherine's brother, giving news of Mr and Mrs Morland's blessing on James' proposal of marriage to Isabella Thorpe, Catherine's particular Bath-time friend (p. 135). There is even reference to a letter written by Catherine herself, to her parents, seeking permission to accompany the Tilneys to Northanger Abbey, their Gloucestershire home:

> 'I will write home directly,' said she, 'and if they do not object, as I dare say they will not' – (. . .)
>
> . . . with spirits elated to rapture, with Henry at her heart, and Northanger Abbey on her lips, she hurried home to write her letter.
>
> (p. 149)

We learn a lot about what (and the way in which) Catherine thinks from what she says. There is a lot of direct speech in *Northanger Abbey*. But – though Jane Austen writes in the third person – we also learn a lot about what (and how) Catherine thinks from the fact that Jane Austen tells us the entire story very much from Catherine's point of view. So we may very easily imagine what sort of a letter she might have written.

Alternative English

 You could write the letter that Catherine might have written to her parents in Chapter 17, soliciting their approval for her reception at Northanger Abbey; *or* you could write a letter from Catherine to her sister and confidante, Sally, telling her about her meeting with James, their brother, and the 'odious' John Thorpe (Chapter 7).

If Catherine had been the heroine of convention, about what other events, meetings, feelings or fears might she have written to Sally?

Again, this is a 'creative' assignment, so you would need to add to the letter an explanation of, and rationale for, its contents.

Alternatively, you might write an extract from the journal that a conventional heroine would have written, that Catherine perhaps wrote, and perhaps did not.

3 An alternative ending

How does an author know when to bring a novel to an end?

There should be no loose ends: we need to know, by the time we put a novel down, what has become of (at least) the major characters to whom we have been introduced, and events that seemed important at the time (that were perhaps the climaxes at chapter endings) must be shown to have had some significance when the plot has been unfolded. A novel of this tidy sort is rather like a symphony: the subjects have been fully worked out, there have been changes of tempo and tone colour, and the finale is in the home-key. It is grand and final.

Many modern novels, however, are not symphonic. They are not sagas or chronicles with a beginning, middle and end. They are studies, slices of life, as *un*tidy and *un*finished as life is. Many short stories do not end on a punch line; they fade out, like a popular song.

Many of Katherine Mansfield's stories (*Selected Stories*, OUP, The World's Classics) may appear to fade out in this way. 'The Garden-Party', for example, takes us to a large country-house. There is to be a garden-party, with a marquee and a band, on the lawns. Laura, a daughter of the house, makes friends with the workmen setting up the marquee, and makes light of 'absurd class distinctions'. Then she hears that a man has died in an accident down the hill from the front gates. At first, Laura wants to cancel the garden-party, but she is persuaded to visit the man's family when it is over. She does so, taking a basket of party food with her. She is awed by the meanness of the cottage in which the young man has been laid; and she is awed by his asleep-seeming, so peaceful corpse. On her way back to the house, she meets her brother Laurie:

> *He stepped out of the shadow. 'Is that you, Laura?'*
> *'Yes.'*
> *'Mother was getting anxious. Was it all right?'*
> *'Yes, quite. Oh, Laurie!' She took his arm, she pressed up against him.*
> *'I say, you're not crying are you?' asked her brother. Laura shook her head. She was.*
> *Laurie put his arm round her shoulder. 'Don't cry,' he said in his warm, loving voice. 'Was it awful?'*
> *'No,' sobbed Laura. 'It was simply marvellous. But, Laurie –'*
> *She stopped, she looked at her brother. 'Isn't life,' she stammered, 'isn't life –' But what life was she couldn't explain. No matter. He quite understood.*
> *'Isn't it, darling?' said Laurie.*
>
> OUP edition, p. 251

Could the story have ended in any other way? One cannot explain what life is in a short story.

Reggie (in 'Mr and Mrs Dove') is about to return to his lonely life in Rhodesia, but before he goes he means to propose to Anne, the popular, beautiful, clever daughter of Colonel Proctor. He excuses himself from his mother's jealous company, and walks to the house in prayerful trepidation. Anne receives him. Reggie is awkward; but Anne finds him amusing – she always has done. She shows him her doves, and explains that Mr Dove always follows Mrs Dove. Mrs Dove always gives a little 'laugh' and Mr Dove follows her, bowing and bowing. At last Reggie asks Anne to marry him – but all she can do is to laugh. It is impossible, she says; they would be like Mr and Mrs Dove. Reggie is cast down at her words, whilst she is bewildered by the misery to which her words have reduced him.

> *'Even if I can't marry you, how can I know that you're all that way away, with only that awful mother to write to, and that you're miserable, and that it's all my fault?'*
> *'It's not your fault. Don't think that. It's just fate.'*
> *Reggie took her hand off his sleeve and kissed it. 'Don't pity me, dear little Anne,' he said gently. And this time he nearly ran, under the pink arches, along the garden path.*
> *'Roo-coo-coo-coo! Roo-coo-coo-coo!' sounded from the veranda. 'Reggie, Reggie' from the garden.*

He stopped, he turned. But when she saw his timid, puzzled look, she gave a little laugh.

'Come back, Mr Dove,' said Anne. And Reginald came slowly across the lawn.

(p. 281)

 The story *could* have ended differently. Or it could have gone on. What would Reggie say to his mother? What would he say to Colonel Proctor? What reasons would Anne give for having (apparently) changed her mind? Why did Katherine Mansfield leave the story where she did?

You could write:

either

1. an alternative ending to one or other of the above two stories – you could, that is, go back and supply quite another outcome to earlier events;

or

2. you could add a further development to either of these stories, or to any other in the collection.

Again, you would need to explain why you feel your ending is true to Katherine Mansfield's beginning. Your writing would need to grow organically out of hers, and be shown to do so.

Alternatively, you could write about Katherine Mansfield's endings in general. Is there a pattern to them that you can discern?

---

4 The film of the book

The British film director Sir David Lean supplied an alternative ending for his version of E. M. Forster's *A Passage to India*. He said his aim in the film was:

> ... not to come down on the side of the English or the Indians, but to be fair to both. In Forster's book all the men are complete idiots, but in fact the British in India did a damned good job. The demands of the film as a medium meant that I had to change the ending, and I've also swung the balance against the women because I believe that old saying about it being the women who lost us the Empire.
>
> *Radio Times*, 26 March–1 April 1988

These words were quoted by Sheridan Morley in the piece that appeared in the *Radio Times* in the week in which Lean's film was shown on BBC television. Lean had been so disappointed by the television broadcast of his film *The Bridge on the River Kwai* (based on the novel by Pierre Boulle), that he made *A Passage to India* with the small screen in mind. That is to say, he preferred close-ups to panoramas.

7.15pm
A Passage to India

FILM

The Academy Award-winning feature film starring
Judy Davis
as Adela Quested
Victor Banergee
as Dr Aziz
Peggy Ashcroft
as Mrs Moore
James Fox
as Richard Fielding
Nigel Havers
as Ronny Heaslop
and **Alec Guinness**
as Professor Godbole

India, the 1920s: Adela Quested is in Chandrapore to visit her fiancé Ronny Heaslop. Through Mr Fielding, the principal of Government College, she and her companion Mrs Moore are introduced to Dr Aziz, a Muslim surgeon. Anxious to please the two western women, Aziz organises a trip to the fabulous Marabar Caves. When Adela goes off alone to explore, events take a terrifying turn...

This magnificent adaptation of the novel by E.M. Forster is brought to the screen by the great British director David Lean, who celebrated his 80th birthday last month.

Turton..............RICHARD WILSON
Mrs Turton
            ANTONIA PEMBERTON
McBryde........MICHAEL CULVER
Mahmoud Ali..........ART MALIK
Hamidullah.......SAEED JAFFREY
Major Callender ...CLIVE SWIFT
Mrs Callender...ANN FAIRBANK
Amritrao................ROSHAN SETH

Radio Times,
26 March–1 April 1988

Lean did not only 'change the ending' of Forster's story, he made a significant change to the events recounted in Chapter 8. After the tea-party at Fielding's house, Ronny drops Mrs Moore off at home, and takes Adela to see a polo game. There, Adela gives tentative voice to her decision not to marry Ronny. He is hurt, but he is understanding. There seems to be nothing to discuss. Adela is relieved to have said her piece. She says:

> 'We've been awfully British over it, but I suppose that's all right.'
> 'As we are British, I suppose it is.'
> 'Anyhow we've not quarrelled, Ronny.'
> 'Oh, that would have been too absurd. Why should we quarrel?'
> 'I think we shall keep friends.'
> 'I know we shall.'
> 'Quite so.'

Penguin edition, p. 83

At this point, the 'loyal' Indian Nawab Bahadur offers to take Ronny and Adela for a spin in his car. They accept his offer. As the car bumps along the Marabar Road:

> *Ronny's face grew dim – an event which always increased her esteem for his character. Her hand touched his, owing to a jolt, and one of the thrills so frequent in the animal kingdom passed between them, and announced that all their difficulties were only a lovers' quarrel.*
>
> (pp. 85–6)

The car runs into an animal (a hyena?), and comes to a stop against a tree. Happily, Miss Derek approaches in a car bearing the inscription of her employer, the Maharajah of Mudkul State. She takes Ronny, Adela and the Nawab Bahadur back into Chandrapore. By the time they have arrived back at the bungalow, the quarrel is a thing of the past.

> *They looked at each other when they reached the bungalow, for Mrs Moore was inside it. It was for Miss Quested to speak, and she said nervously, 'Ronny, I should like to take back what I said on the Maidan.' He assented, and they became engaged to be married in consequence.*
>
> (p. 91)

How does Sir David Lean capture this change of heart? He has Adela (presumably on the day following the polo game) cycle on her own along paths and field edges to a ruined Hindu temple, half-hidden among trees and high grasses. There she gazes on the sculpted limbs of lovers in abandoned poses – a stone Kama Sutra – until she is frightened away by hordes of chattering monkeys. Adela has seen enough, however, so that by the time she meets Ronny, as she garages her bicycle, the animal has overcome the intellectual in her, and she withdraws her disengaging words of the Maidan.

Lean's version of events is less subtle than Forster's, but perhaps 'film as a medium' is unable to capture the subtlety of the written word. Little is lost in the alteration, except that we see rather less of the Nawab Bahadur in the film than we do in the book, and Forster explains how it is that Miss Derek is driving in the vicinity of the Marabar Caves, just when Adela needs her most, where Lean does not.

Sir Alec Guinness, who played Professor Godbole, wondered whether Forster would be 'rejoicing or revolving in his grave'. It is my view, having read the novel several times and seen the film twice, that if Lean did not observe the letter of the novel, he most certainly observed its spirit.

When we see the film of a novel we know well, we are inclined to ask ourselves what has been added, what has been omitted, and why. And whether the changes are for the better or the worse.

You could ask yourselves these questions of David Lean's film.

Alternatively, you could take him up on the points he made, quoted above: that he wanted 'to be fair to both' the English and the Indians, and that 'In Forster's book all the men are complete idiots.' *Was* Lean fair to both groups? Was Forster *not* fair to one or the other of them? Is Fielding, for example, a 'complete idiot'? Can this be said even of Ronny?

5 Dramatisation

A play was made of *A Passage to India* for the West End stage in the 1960s. Here there was no mosque and there were no caves. All that needed to be said about what had happened on Dr Aziz's ill-fated expedition had to be said at the Club or in the Courtroom.

Virtually all of Dickens' novels have been dramatised, whether for the big screen, the small screen or the stage. *Hard Times* is a novel much studied, but little performed. It has never achieved the popularity of his other, London-based, North Kent novels. Perhaps it is that the novelist's want of familiarity with Preston (Coketown) shows; perhaps too few of the characters (and Stephen Blackpool and Rachael, in particular) are really credible; or perhaps Dickens allows argument to dominate story.

The novels of Dickens are peculiarly adaptable to the stage. Dickens himself was a keen amateur actor, and he was in demand for his full-bodied readings of the most suspenseful passages from his novels. His novels contain dramatic – not to say, melodramatic – scenes. There is the scene, for instance, in which Stephen's wife reaches for the poison at her bedside. Stephen and Rachael are present in the dark room, keeping sleepy watch.

> ... *she laid her insensate grasp upon the bottle that had swift and certain death in it, and, before his eyes, pulled out the cork with her teeth.*
>
> *Dream or reality, he had no voice, nor had he power to stir. If this be real, and her allotted time be not yet come, wake, Rachael, wake!*
>
> *She thought of that, too. She looked at Rachael, and very slowly, very cautiously, poured out the contents. The draught was at her lips. A moment and she would be*

> *past all help, let the whole world wake and come about her with its utmost power. But, in that moment Rachael started up with a suppressed cry. The creature struggled, struck her, seized her by the hair; but Rachael had the cup.*
>
> Penguin edition, p. 124

And there is powerful dialogue. Much of the raw material of the dramatisation, or the screenplay, is already there – and it's there from the start. Mr Gradgrind interrogates Sissy Jupe, in the schoolroom, in Chapter 2.

> *'Girl number twenty,' said Mr Gradgrind, squarely pointing with his square forefinger, 'I don't know that girl. Who is that girl?'*
>
> *'Sissy Jupe, sir,' explained number twenty, blushing, standing up, and curtseying.*
>
> *'Sissy is not a name,' said Mr Gradgrind. 'Don't call yourself Sissy. Call yourself Cecilia.'*
>
> *'It's father as calls me Sissy, sir,' returned the young girl in a trembling voice, and with another curtsey.*
>
> *'Then he has no business to do it,' said Mr Gradgrind. 'Tell him he mustn't. Cecilia Jupe. Let me see. What is your father?'*
>
> *'He belongs to the horse-riding, if you please, sir.'*
>
> *Mr Gradgrind frowned, and waved off the objectionable calling with his hand.*
>
> *'We don't want to know anything about that here.'*
>
> (p. 49)

The Welsh Theatre Company, Theatr Powys, made a two-hour play of *Hard Times*, and set it in Sleary's Circus. Iola Smith reviewed the production for *The Times Educational Supplement*. Evidently there were messages in it beyond those intended by Dickens – and it was presumably none the worse for that.

Lifeline

Hard Times.
Theatr Powys.

On the day that Kenneth Baker announced the establishment of new technical schools, Theatr Powys gave vocational education a punch on the nose by presenting the shortcomings of its 19th-century caricature, the Gradgrind system in Dickens' *Hard Times*.

'Education should not be for work, but for life,' said writer Greg Cullen. 'Too much of our schooling denies human potential.' Calling for more creativity and 'learning through feeling' was the essence of his adaptation of the novel. The plot was simplified and condensed into two-and-a-half hours. Setting it in a circus both unified the action – the narrative was kept flowing by the circus folk – and emphasized the importance of learning through entertainment.

The play was a potted guide to the Victorian class structure ranging from Gradgrind to the wronged and much-maligned weaver, Stephen Blackpool. Just six actors played all the parts: a change of voice and jacket saw lisping circus owner Sleary (John Ballanger) transformed into the confident banker Bounderby. Walking on stilts, he became the tyrannical teacher M'Choakumchild, towering over terrified children.

The play is being performed throughout Wales and the border counties. But unless more funding is forthcoming, this may be Theatr Powys' last national tour. Times are hard for the company as well as the citizens of Coketown, and the play could be viewed as an eloquent plea for the continued survival of TIE as an art form in schools.

Iola Smith

The Times Educational Supplement,
24 November 1986

One of the major themes of the novel is the opposition between what is free, and natural, and what is disciplined and regimented. The circus is the appropriate place for an emphasis on the former.

You could dramatise (part of) the novel, and set it in the 'plain, bare, monotonous vault of a schoolroom', or in 'the forest of looms' in the hot mill. In either of these places, you would lay emphasis on regimentation, on 'facts', and on 'man and masters'.

Bounderby's house is another possibility, or Bounderby's Bank.

Confine yourself to one aspect of the plot or sub-plot, and feel free to draw upon as much, or as little, of the novel as seems appropriate.

As before, supply a brief interpretative commentary with your scene as a variant form of 'criticism'.

6 The writer's life and work

The student of the novel is not required to know anything at all about the novelist. Critics have not, on the whole, been concerned with where, when or how the author lived. They have not regarded it as the business of literary criticism to inquire into the author's circumstances; they leave this to biographers and – where more modern novelists are concerned – to gossip columnists.

There is written 'work', however, that cannot altogether be understood when set apart from the writer's 'life'. A background knowledge of Jane Austen's life and times may not be *necessary* to an intelligent reading of *Northanger Abbey* (or any other of her novels), but it helps. Some familiarity with the factory system, with the patriarchal family, and with Dickens' own experience of poverty and a loveless marriage *must* add to an understanding of the 'message' of *Hard Times*. We cannot read Katherine Mansfield's New Zealand stories ('The Voyage', for example, and 'At the Bay') without reference to the reasons for her nostalgia arising from the death of her brother, and her own fatal condition.

To know that his father drank, that his mother sang, and that he himself was destined to be a Roman Catholic priest is information of some relevance to interpretation of 'Grace', 'A Mother', and 'The Sisters' (respectively), by James Joyce. His *Dubliners* are people James Joyce knew in the city of his birth, childhood and youth. A number of the characters try to escape from the city, from its counting-house desks, from its confession-box morals, and its Gaelic chauvinism. We will not make much of references to 'paralysis', and 'simony', to the 'Catholic wine-merchant's office', to 'old jog-along Dublin', the 'language movement', 'Terry Kelly's pawn-office', and 'the magic-lantern business', if we do not know that these were features of Dublin, and of *Dubliners*, from which James Joyce himself was a refugee. We will not know why the 'themes of repression, entrapment and revolt' run all the way through *Dubliners* (as we are told they do on the rear cover of the Granada edition) if we do not know why Joyce thought of Dublin as a trap from which he must escape.

'A Little Cloud' is the story of Little Chandler, a sensitive would-be poet, a married man, and a clerk at the King's Inns. He has a drink one evening with an old school friend, Ignatius Gallaher. Already, Little Chandler has concluded: 'if you wanted to succeed you had to go away. You could do nothing in Dublin.' Gallaher had got away; he was a journalist on the 'London Press'. Little Chandler goes to meet Gallaher at Corless's, a high-class bar where the waiters speak French and German. He is dressed up, and as he walks to the bar down mean streets, he feels superior to those he passes. Over a watered whisky, he invites Gallaher home to meet his wife. Gallaher excuses himself.

'For the first time in his life he felt himself superior to the people he passed.'

He felt acutely the contrast between his own life and his friend's, and it seemed to him unjust. Gallaher was his inferior in birth and education. He was sure that he could do something better than his friend had ever done, or could ever do, something higher than mere tawdry journalism if he only got the chance. What was it that stood in his way? His unfortunate timidity! He wished to vindicate himself in some way, to assert his manhood. He saw behind Gallaher's refusal of his invitation. Gallaher was only patronising him by his friendliness just as he was patronising Ireland by his visit.

Granada edition, p. 73

'The Dead' is the last story in the collection, almost of novella length. John Huston has made a well-reviewed film of the story, about Gabriel Conroy and his part in the Misses Morkans' annual dance. He is a genial, if at times 'pitiable fatuous fellow'. He is awkward with the caretaker's daughter, and the butt of jokes for his 'solicitude' towards his family. But what really unsettles him is an altercation with a colleague, a Miss Ivors, on the dance-floor. She asks him to join her, and others, on an excursion to the Aran Isles. Gabriel, however, has other plans:

> —Well, you know, every year I go for a cycling tour with some fellows, and so –
> —But where? asked Miss Ivors.
> —Well, we usually go to France or Belgium or perhaps Germany, said Gabriel awkwardly.
> —And why do you go to France and Belgium, said Miss Ivors, instead of visiting your own land?
> —Well, said Gabriel, it's partly to keep in touch with the languages and partly for a change.
> —And haven't you your own language to keep in touch with – Irish? asked Miss Ivors.
> —Well, said Gabriel, if it comes to that, you know, Irish is not my language (. . .)
> —And haven't you your own land to visit, continued Miss Ivors, that you know nothing of, your own people, and your own country?
> —Oh, to tell you the truth, retorted Gabriel suddenly, I'm sick of my own country, sick of it!
>
> (p. 171)

Gabriel has booked a room in a local hotel for the night. He hopes to have contrived an atmosphere in which he might spend his passion with his wife, Gretta. It is the irony of the story that it is 'Ireland' that thwarts his passion. Gretta has heard Mr D'Arcy singing 'The Lass of Aughrim', and this has put her in mind of a boy who died for love of her. Gabriel's love is made to seem tawdry and self-serving by comparison.

 Are Little Chandler and Gabriel Conroy alternative names for James Joyce himself?

Find out about some of the main features of the life of James Joyce, then determine how many of those features are mirrored in *Dubliners*.

In what sense are the themes of 'repression, entrapment and revolt' identifiable in Joyce's life? How does he give vent to them in (this) 'work'? (You could confine yourself to a consideration of Little Chandler in 'A Little Cloud', or to Gabriel Conroy, in 'The Dead'; or you could range more widely.)

---

7 The writer's 'message'

We ask what a novel is about. We are bound to. Yet few novelists will want to give a straight answer to the question. Still fewer will want to talk in terms of 'messages', as if their novels were statements, or fables with a moral. If novelists had something of a social, or political, or philosophical, or moral sort to say, they would be journalists, or essay-writers, or broadcasters.

Some, of course, are. There has always been a busy two-way traffic between journalism and fiction – and, most recently, between the novel and 'the media'. George Orwell did write essays, and works of a socio-political kind; and he would have been aggrieved if *Animal Farm* had been read as no more than a story about animals in revolt.

Nineteen Eighty-Four, too, has a message so strong that Orwell's name is given to a nightmare. That the novel is 'about' totalitarianism is beyond doubt; but precisely what the message of the novel is – what Orwell would have us understand the nature of the prophecy to be – is open to interpretation. At least three films (one of them for television) have been made of the novel. According to John Coleman in the *New Statesman* (opposite), had the same cinema-goer seen the film of 1955 and that of 1984, he or she might have been forgiven for thinking that they were film-versions of two different novels.

John Hurt's Winston dreams of Richard Burton's O'Brien as a father figure

> THAT IT HAS been brought in and put out in the commercially appropriate year is already an achievement. But that **Nineteen Eighty-Four**, scripted and directed by Michael Radford, produced by Simon Perry, should have been so finely brought off is something else again. After Michael Anderson's 1955 film version, so 'freely adapted from George Orwell' as to cast a paunchy Edmund O'Brien as the doomed Winston Smith and then to mar that doom by an up-beat shout of 'Down with Big Brother' as bullets thudded home, Sonia Orwell was rightly distressed and, on the expiry of Warners' rights in 1974, would brook no further showing of the travesty.
>
> Somehow, a movie-mad American lawyer Marvin Rosenblum worked on her so that, before her death at the end of 1980, she gave him TV rights and a film option on the awkward fiction. For it was a bothersome, misunderstood novel from the moment of its publication. Some saw it as pure anti-Communist propaganda, some ('Ingsoc') as a smack at our domestic Labour Party: only the alert recognised it as a harshly satiric warning against totalitarianism anywhere and, notably, as a klaxon loudly sounding against verbal traffic-jams with an inevitable simplification of language to the point of readily adjusted sloganism, mental serfdom.
>
> *New Statesman*, 12 October 1984

The Great Gatsby by F. Scott Fitzgerald is unlikely ever to have been thought 'a bothersome, misunderstood novel'. It seems on the contrary to be a limpidly clear account of a tragic romance. It has been hailed as a critique of the illusion and glamour of 'The Jazz Age'. The plot is pure melodrama: there is adultery, there is fabulous excess, there is a mystery about identity, there is a whiff of organised crime, there is argument, accident, unrelenting heat, and revenge killing. There is poetry, there is style, there is personality, and there is atmosphere of period and place. Angela Carter, herself a novelist, puts it rather well (in the extract from the article below) when she calls *The Great Gatsby* a 'romance of high capitalism'. She goes on to identify the hero of the novel, and to say something of what (in her view) it is about:

NOVEL CHOICE

An occasional series in which authors and critics discuss one of their favourite works of fiction

Angela Carter on

THE GREAT GATSBY

by F. Scott Fitzgerald

'The Great Gatsby' is a romance, perhaps the most perfect romance, of high capitalism, which may be one of the reasons why the novel has proved so easy to merchandise. Because Fitzgerald is so upfront and unembarrassed – 'Her voice is full of money' – about this love story which is poignant solely because each word, each gesture, each caress of the two principals is determined by economic factors, it is easy to forget that he is but rehearsing a universal truth and doing so with a peculiar and remorseless lucidity.

And it is one of the great middle-brow classics – a soft-edge production, in no way intellectually demanding: you lie back and have it done to you. It is a ravishing novel; but it does not ravish you to no purpose.

Indeed, in spite of its small scale, though it is the smallness of scale that helps give 'Gatsby' its odd illusion of perfection, it is the most Balzacian of all American novels and certainly the only authentic American account of a sentimental education that I know of. Not that it is Gatsby who is thus educated: it is the narrator, Nick Carraway, who is the hero of the novel, and who acquires almost too much weary knowledge of the heart at Gatsby's expense. Gatsby himself is no hero. He is the dupe of the dream. Reality would spoil things.

So 'Gatsby' is about *not* making it, about the intractability of social class, about the yawning gulf between wealth and money and that between love and marriage.

The Observer Magazine,
24 February 1980

You could say what *you* believe either of the above two novels is 'about' – what you take the writer's essential 'message' in either case to be.

Alternatively, you could take up certain of the points made by the above two critics:

1 *Nineteen Eighty-Four*: What makes it an 'awkward', 'bothersome' book? Is it 'notably' a warning against the 'simplification of language', as Coleman suggests. What other warnings does it sound? Does Orwell's novel still have a 'message' for today?
2 *The Great Gatsby*: What (on earth) does Angela Carter mean when she calls the novel: 'one of the great middlebrow classics'? What is the 'yawning gulf between wealth and money'? What 'message' does Fitzgerald appear to issue about 'love and marriage'?

8 A line to the author

Angela Carter went on in the article quoted above:

> *The Great Gatsby* is put together with a knife and fork. Formal qualities were never Fitzgerald's strong suit...
>
> (*The Observer Magazine,* 24 February 1980)

Critics, and critical novelists, have always been rather more interested in the 'formal qualities' of a novel than most readers – even than most students of the novel. *The Great Gatsby* was put together by a poet: that is what matters. *Nineteen Eighty-Four* was put together by a prophet – and it is the prophecy that matters. The manner of speaking is not insignificant; it does matter how a novel sounds, how its parts fit together, how its themes are developed, whether the mood is appropriate, whether there is internal consistency and a planned shape – and in practice, the matter and the manner of a novel work together. The how will not be disentangled from the what.

All the same, a novel stands or falls, survives or dies, in proportion to the depth, breadth and height of its ideas. *The Go-Between* is a well-made novel, and it will survive. But it is not prophecy, in the sense that *The Trial, Nineteen Eighty-Four, Lord of the Flies* and *Schindler's Ark* are prophecies. I will not 'teach' the last-named of these novels (a 'documentary' novel by Thomas Keneally about a German industrialist in Nazi-occupied Poland and his heroic defence of his Jewish work-force against the authorities – and his own interests) because the subject-matter – its *donné* – transcends all consideration of its 'formal qualities'.

Ngugi's *Petals of Blood* is another such. It is not necessary to have read a score of other novels about post-independence Africa to recognise that this one is a major novel by any standard. This is not merely because Ngugi used imagery to powerful effect – that he is a fabulist, like the great Nigerian Chinua Achebe and the Ghanaian Ayi Kwei Armah. The novel's real power is in its author's controlled passion. It is a novel 'about' the betrayal of the Kenyan revolution against white colonialism by black colonials wearing English wigs and driving German cars. It is about four outsiders who settle in Ilmorog with a view to building in the village a microcosm of the brave new Kenya. Abdulla is one of the four. He lost a leg in the freedom-movement; he fought with the hero Kimathi. Then, after the struggle, he waited for the better times for which he had fought. He says, himself:

Ngugi Wa Thiongo

'I waited for land reforms and redistribution.

'I waited for a job.

'I waited for a statue to Kimathi as a memorial to the fallen.

'I waited.

'I said to myself, let me sell half an acre of my one acre. I did: I bought myself a donkey and a cart. I became a transporter of people's goods in the market. A donkey does not drink petrol or kerosene.

'Still I waited.

'I heard that they were giving loans for people to buy out European farms. I did not see why I should buy land, already bought by the blood of the people. Still I went there. They told me: this is New Kenya. No free things. Without money you cannot buy land: and without land and property you cannot get a bank loan to start business or buy land. It did not make sense. For when we were fighting, did we ask that only those with property should fight?

'I said, maybe, maybe . . . a master plan . . .

'I waited.

'I thought O.K., I will become dumb. I will become deaf; I watched

> *things unfold. Happenings. I saw the mounting tension between black people. This and that community. Between regions. Ridges even. Between homes. And I remembered our struggle, our fight, our songs: for didn't I carry the memory on my leg? I said: why this and that between our peoples? The white man: won't he now laugh and laugh until his nose splits into two like the louse in the story?'*

Heinemann AWS edition, p. 254

The black banks and businesses and big men take over Ilmorog and the modest dreams of the four (other) outsiders, in rather the same way that the pigs take over Animal Farm.

Petals of Blood (like Orwell's fable) is a novel about disillusionment, that is all the deeper for the way in which Ngugi, relentlessly, shows Abdulla's and the others' dreams to be flawed also. Each longs for a New World (Marxist or evangelical) that fails to come to grips with this one. A novelist who was imprisoned without charge has a right to his indignation. He cannot have found release in easy answers.

Still, we do ask questions. You might have considered writing to an author of a set book to seek clarification from the horse's mouth, but you have probably not written. Nevertheless, many authors do receive letters from students, asking them (in various ways) what their work is 'about'. It is normally only given to biographers, journalists and PhD students to interview them.

 You could write to Ngugi (he lives in London now), asking him questions about *Petals of Blood* – why it is so pessimistic; whether he is himself best represented in the person of Abdulla, or Munira, or Karega.

Or you could write to Chinua Achebe, to ask him questions about *Arrow of God* – searching questions that reveal your own close knowledge and (at least partial) understanding of (part of) the novel.

Or you could 'interview' Ngugi (or Achebe), basing his 'answers' on the language and point of view of one of the main characters of the novel.

TWO

Plays

What is a play?

A novel has to be fiction in order that it is not non-fiction, and therefore not a novel. Does a play have to be *fiction*?

Robert Bolt's play *A Man for All Seasons* was first produced at the Globe Theatre, London, in 1960; and it was published in a school edition by Heinemann Educational Books in the same year. The rear cover of the paperback version bears these words:

> Thomas More was the pivot of English life at a time when England was negotiating the sharpest corner in her spiritual history, and in this play Robert Bolt gives us a 'life' of this great man whose public and private reputations were staggeringly high. More had no petty enemies, only great and fatal ones, and the drama of his struggle with these enemies forms the basis of this outstanding play.
>
> **Robert Bolt** has written a play of historical accuracy that ends in 1535, and yet it is one of the most significant plays of our time. Paul Scofield gave a masterful portrayal of Sir Thomas More in the first London stage production at the Globe Theatre, which he repeated in Columbia's magnificent film.
>
> Heinemann Educational edition, rear cover

That's an interesting 'yet' in the second paragraph: the play is accurate *yet* significant. The implication is that if Bolt had departed from the historical record (as Jean Anouilh, the French playwright, did in his play about St Joan, *L'Alouette*) his play might have been still more significant.

Art is generally reckoned to consist in interpretation, not accuracy. A photo-realist portrait may not be rated highly as art.

Bolt himself, in his Preface to the play, wrote as follows:

> *I set out with no very well-formed idea of the kind of play it was to be, except that it was not to be naturalistic . . . if, as I think, a play is more like a poem than a straight narration, still less a demonstration or lecture, then imagery ought to be important.*

And so Bolt used imagery. Throughout the play he used the image of the sea and water for 'the superhuman context'; and for society, he used the image of dry land. Thomas More did not use those images; nor did Henry VIII. To this extent, Bolt departed from historical accuracy. We do not ask whether a poem is fiction or non-fiction: the question does not arise. If a play is more like a poem than a straight history, as Bolt contends, we should not, perhaps, ask the question of plays either.

Of course, even if Bolt *had* wanted to write history, he would not have written an accurate record if all it consisted of was dialogue. There was no record made of More's conversations with his family, or with Cromwell, or with his king. However true to More's written words Bolt might have been, and whatever use he made of the transcript of his trial (if there is such a thing), most of the dialogue in the play must be Bolt's own.

A play must have *dialogue* (or monologue) or it is *mime*, and not a play at all. The lines might rhyme, or be otherwise in verse (blank verse, or free), as the plays of T. S. Eliot are:

> MESSENGER
> *Servants of God, and watchers of the temple,*
> *I am here to inform you, without circumlocution:*
> *The Archbishop is in England, and is close outside the city.*
> *I was sent before in haste*
> *To give you notice of his coming, as much as was possible,*
> *That you may prepare to meet him.*
>
> FIRST PRIEST
> *What, is the exile ended, is our Lord Archbishop*
> *Reunited with the King? What reconciliation*
> *Of two proud men?*
>
> THIRD PRIEST
> *What peace can be found*
> *To grow between the hammer and the anvil?*
>
> Murder in the Cathedral, Part I, Faber edition, p. 26

No one has ever accused Shakespeare's tragedies of not being plays because Othello, Macbeth, Hamlet and King Lear speak in blank verse. So we are not disturbed in plays, as we are in novels, by whether or not they are in prose.

If we are not disturbed by poetry, will we be disturbed by song? *Oklahoma!*, *The Boy Friend*, *West Side Story* – we call these musical drama, or just musicals. We don't think of them as 'plays', and we would be surprised if they were set for study, as literature.

Oh What a Lovely War combines dialogue with songs, and slides, and a 'newspanel' delivering facts and statistics. These run into each other without a break:

> LANDRU. *Excusez-moi, s'il vous plaît.*
> GENDARME. *Hey! M. Landru! Where are you going with that body?*
> LANDRU. *I am going to bury it. With all this killing going on and they never called me up, I thought I'd settle a few private scores.*
> GENDARME. *Good idea! ... How many have you done?*
> LANDRU. *Twelve wives, so far.*
> GENDARME. *Hey! Just a minute. You're for the guillotine.*
>
> Both go off.
>
> NEWSPANEL. NOVEMBER...SOMME BATTLE ENDS...TOTAL LOSS 1,322,000 MEN... GAIN NIL.
>
> The band plays a few bars of 'Twelfth Street Rag'. Three couples dance wildly and continue as the soldier in uniform sings:
>
> SONG   I WORE A TUNIC
>   (Tune: 'I wore a Tulip')
> *I wore a tunic, a dirty khaki tunic,*
> *And you wore your civvy clothes,*
> *We fought and bled at Loos, while you were on the booze.*
> *The booze that no one here knows.*
> *You were out with the wenches, while we were in the trenches,*
>   etc.
>
> Eyre Methuen edition, p. 93

Is this a play, or a musical comedy, or a pageant, or what? On the reverse of the title page there is a:

> NOTE TO THE READER
> *This is a play script and should be read as such.*

As with the novel, it would seem that a play is a play if the playwright, the publisher or reviewer says it is.

It does not quite go without saying that a play must have characters, because there are plays that have only one character (or one speaking character). A play without anyone in it at all would be no more than *son et lumière*.

Finally, among the supposed requirements of a play is *action*, or *plot*. Something must happen, one would think; there must be some story, some sequence of events, so that – just as the reader of a novel wants to know what happens next – the audience at a play wants to know how the plot will unfold.

Samuel Beckett is famous for stripping a play to the minimum. In *Endgame* (1958) Hamm sits in a chair because he cannot stand up, Clov walks backwards and forwards because he cannot sit down, and Hamm's mother and father cannot do either, because each is confined in a dustbin. Hamm's mother dies, it seems, in her dustbin towards the end of the play, and Clov stops coming and going and dresses up to go for good. But nothing can be said to happen. There are some good lines – even amusing lines:

> HAMM. *This is deadly.*
>   Enter Clov with telescope. He goes towards ladder.
> CLOV. *Things are livening up.* (He gets up on ladder, raises the telescope, lets it fall.) *I did it on purpose* (He gets down, picks up the telescope, turns it on auditorium.) *I see a multitude . . . in transports . . . of joy.* (Pause.) *That's what I call a magnifier.* (He lowers the telescope, turns towards Hamm.) *Well? Don't we laugh?*
> HAMM. (after reflection) *I don't.*
> CLOV. (after reflection) *Nor I.* (He gets up on ladder, turns the telescope on the without.) *Let's see.* (He looks, moving the telescope.) *Zero . . .* (he looks) *. . . zero . . .* (he looks) *. . . and zero.*
> HAMM. *Nothing stirs. All is –*
> CLOV. *Zer-*
> HAMM. (violently) *Wait till you're spoken to!*
>
> Faber edition, p. 25

It is a play of deep meanings – and of none at all. Hamm both strives for meaning, and resists it.

> HAMM. *We're not beginning to . . . to . . . mean something?*
> CLOV. *Mean something! You and I, mean something!* (Brief laugh) *Ah that's a good one.*
>
> (p. 27)

There is movement, there is some stage-business, there are some scraps of stories, and there is a complete 'joke' – but there is no *plot*.

What do we look for in a play?

It was said in Chapter One that for a novel to be 'significant', either its subject *matter* had to be of some importance, or it had to be written in such a *manner* as in some way to advance the art of the novel. Thus Huxley's *Brave New World* might be said to be significant on the first count, and Dorothy Richardson's *Pointed Roofs* (1915) on the second. (Virginia Woolf was indebted to Dorothy Richardson for her use of the stream-of-consciousness technique.)

If this was an over-simplification where the novel is concerned, it is probably an over-simplification in respect of the play. The best writers in any form meld *content* and *form* in such a way that matter and manner are indissoluble.

Still, it is probably true to say that a play of some substance speaks to its time, and a 'great' play speaks to all time.

Shelagh Delaney's *A Taste of Honey* spoke to its time. The year was 1959, and the playwright was aged 20. The play spoke about Salford's working class, about relationships across the 'colour bar', and about the 'new morality' (or sex before marriage). Its portrayal of casual sex, casual parenthood, casual loyalties, was a shock to the system in 1959. It was an anti-establishment play, an angry-young-woman play, whose time had come. It remains a fine achievement, but there is a sense in which the play is dated now.

Arnold Wesker's *Chips with Everything* (1962) is in something of the same category. It is a play 'about' life in the services, about social snobbery, and the high wall between officers and men. Pip is a rebel against his class. He resisted officer training, but succumbs to the inevitable before the final curtain. Corporal Hill does not wish to give new recruits the illusion that this will be a 'cushy' life.

> CORPORAL HILL. *Right, you're in the R.A.F. now, you're not at home. This hut, this place here, this is going to be your home for the next eight scorching weeks. This billet here, you see it? This? It's in a state now, no one's been in it for the last four days so it's in a state now.* (Pause.) *But usually it's like a scorching palace!* (Pause.) *That's the way I want it to be cos that's the way it's always been. Now, you've got to get to know me. My name's Corporal Hill. I'm not a very happy man, I don't know why. I never smile and I never joke – you'll soon see that. Perhaps it's my nature, perhaps it's the way I've been brought up – I don't know. The R.A.F. brought me up. You're going to go through hell while you're here, through scorching hell. Some of you will take it and some of you will break down. I'm warning you – some of you shall end up crying. And when that happens, I don't want to see anyone laughing at him. Leave him alone, don't touch him.*
>
> *But I'll play fair. You do me proud and I'll play fair. The last lot we 'ad 'ere 'ad a good time, a right time, a right good scorching time. We 'ad bags o' fun, bags o' it. But I will tear and mercilessly scratch the scorching daylights out of anyone who smarts the alec with me – and we've got some 'ere. I can see them, you can tell them. I count three already, you can tell them, by their faces, who know it all, the boys who think they're* GOOD. (Whispered.) *It'll be unmerciful and scorching murder for them – all. Now, you see this wireless here, this thing with knobs and*

a pretty light that goes on and off? Well, that's ours, our wireless for this hut and for this hut only because this hut has always been the best hut. No other hut has a wireless. I want to keep it. I like music and I want to keep that wireless. Some people, when they get up in the morning, first thing all they want to do is smoke, or drink tea – not me, I've got to have music, the noise of instruments.

Everyone's got a fad, that's mine, music, and I want to be spoilt, you see to it that I'm spoilt. Right, if there's anyone here who wants to leave my hut and go into another because he doesn't like this 'un, then do it now, please. Go on, pick up your kit and move. I'll let 'im. (No movement.) *You can go to the N.A.A.F.I. now. But be back by ten-thirty, cos that's bleedin' lights out.* (Moves to door, pauses.) *Anyone object to swearing?* (No reply.) (Exits.)

(Stunned, A boy rushes in from another hut.)

BOY. *What's your'n say?*

SMILER (imitating). *My name is Corporal Hill, I'm not a happy man.*

BOY (imitating a Scotsman). *My name is Corporal Bridle – and I'm a bastard!*

BBC Radio edition, pp. 6–7

Hans Schwarz, BBC Radio for Schools, Spring Term, 1967

Corporal Hill is no officer or gentleman. He is one of the other ranks, and he cannot understand Pip, because he is a gentleman yet refuses to be an officer. Snobbery in the services – even class (as opposed to wealth) – is really not an issue any more.

To say that the Delaney and Wesker plays are dated, however, is not to say that they are not worthwhile plays. They could well be revived, and rediscovered by playgoers to whom they will speak all over again.

Brian Friel's *Translations* (1980) has a great deal to say. It is chock-full of matter. It is a set text already because this matter is so timeless and fundamental. The play is set in the County Donegal of 1833, but the place is any colony, the people are any exploited people, and the time is now and then. It is a play 'about' language, and identity, and self-respect, and it speaks through feeling people in words that fairly hum with meanings and double meanings. English soldiers are mapping Ireland, and giving every feature an English name. Owen is helping them, and – in his brother Manus's opinion – betraying his own kind:

> MANUS. (...) What's 'incorrect' about the place-names we have here?
> OWEN. Nothing at all. They're just going to be standardised.
> MANUS. You mean changed into English?
> OWEN. Where there's ambiguity, they'll be Anglicised.
> MANUS. And they call you Roland! They both call you Roland!
> OWEN. Shhhhh. Isn't it ridiculous? They seemed to get it wrong from the beginning – or else they can't pronounce Owen. I was afraid some of you bastards would laugh.
> MANUS. Aren't you going to tell them?
> OWEN. Yes – yes – soon – soon.
> MANUS. But they ...
> OWEN. Easy, man, easy. Owen – Roland – what the hell. It's only a name. It's the same me isn't it? Well, isn't it?
>
> Faber edition, pp. 32–3

Translations is about all that there is in a name. It does not have a strong *story*. It does not depend upon story for its success as, for example, Shaw's *Pygmalion* (1913) does. The 'rags to riches' story is one with universal appeal. What is more, *Pygmalion* is funny. The same can be said of *The Devil's Disciple* (1897). This, again, is not one of Shaw's more serious plays. (Shaw sometimes had a good deal more to say than an entertaining play can bear.) Indeed, he called it a 'melodrama'. More than this, it is a comedy, a romance and a 'historical' play, all in one. David Jones produced a television version of it for the BBC. Hugh David said of the play in the *Radio Times*:

> *The Devil's Disciple* is a romp set during the last days of the American War of Independence. The swashbuckling Dick Dudgeon, the real devil's disciple of the title, is arrested as a rebel in mistake for the real rebel, Pastor Anderson.

7.45 pm
Theatre Night: The Devil's Disciple

by BERNARD SHAW
First in a season of dramas
The American War of Independence is in its second year. Its effects are reaching into the smallest communities, affecting the lives of all in them...

Mrs Dudgeon
    ELIZABETH SPRIGGS
Essie .... CHERYL MAIKER
Christy Dudgeon
    GRAHAM TURNER
Anthony Anderson
    PATRICK STEWART
Judith Anderson
    SUSAN WOOLDRIDGE
Lawyer Hawkins
    PATRICK GODFREY
Uncle William Dudgeon
    PATRICK NEWELL
Mrs William Dudgeon
    FREDA RODGERS
Uncle Titus Dudgeon
    JOHN CATER
Mrs Titus Dudgeon
    JUNE ELLIS
Richard Dudgeon
    MIKE GWILYM
Sergeant .... LARRY LAMB
Major Swindon
    BENJAMIN WHITROW
General Burgoyne
    IAN RICHARDSON
Chaplain
    TIMOTHY KNIGHTLEY
Music composed by STEPHEN OLIVER
Costume designer ODETTE BARROW
Lighting HOWARD KING
Designer TONY BURROUGH
Script editor STUART GRIFFITHS
Producer SHAUN SUTTON
Director DAVID JONES
● FEATURE: *page 14*
★ CEEFAX SUBTITLES

General Burgoyne (Ian Richardson) and Major Swindon (Benjamin Whitrow) prepare the devil's advocate (Mike Gwilym) for his execution on the gallows
BBC2, 7.45 pm Theatre Night: The Devil's Disciple

Radio Times, 16–22 May 1987

Dudgeon is saved from the gallows to go on swashbuckling, and to ensure that the play does not become a tragedy – or worse – a farce.

The Devil's Disciple is something more than just a 'romp'. But plays *have* survived merely by being funny. William Wycherley's *The Country Wife* (1672) is well-plotted – but it makes no pretence to 'significance'. It is a play about rakes, and jealous husbands, and wenching, and intrigue. It is a romp, in fact, as most Restoration comedies were. But this is the best of them (Wycherley's other three comedies have not lasted nearly as well). Perhaps it has lasted because of its period value, and perhaps because it does make for an undemanding, but satisfying, evening's entertainment. Who is to tell?

It will be interesting to see whether Alan Ayckbourn's well-made comedies survive equally well, or whether Joe Orton's bawdy farce *What the Butler Saw* is a set text in years to come.

Perhaps it is already.

How might one write about a play?

1 Adding a scene

It is hard to imagine how one might (or why it should occur to one to) add to a 'well-made' play by Alan Ayckbourn, Robert Bolt or J. B. Priestley. Plays by these writers are self-contained. They are tightly plotted, and have a beginning, middle and end that have a certain pleasing inevitability about them. It is part of the reason for their working that they are not susceptible to bits being cut out of them, or bits being stuck on.

Beckett's *Endgame*, though, is something else again. What intrigues is how Beckett decided where to begin the dialogue (as opposed to the action), and how he decided where to stop it. It's a very surreal sort of life, but *Endgame* is nevertheless a *slice of life* – and Beckett could have cut the slice somewhere else (it might have been thicker or thinner) without doing violence to his dramatic idea.

Harold Pinter was much influenced by Beckett. He has said:

> Beckett is the most courageous, remorseless writer going, and the more he grinds my nose in the shit the more I am grateful to him.

The characters and the situation in *The Caretaker* (1959), especially, owe a great deal to Beckett in whose work the tramp is a stock character. Pinter has said that the shape and the structure – what he calls the 'overall unity' of a play – are of vital importance to him. But it is his dramatic idea (his *donné*) that gives his plays this unity. They are plays from which one could, conceivably, cut quite large chunks, and they are plays to which one could, conceivably, add whole scenes – and to make this claim is in no way to impugn Pinter's skills as a playwright. He has said himself:

> I work much as I write, just moving from one thing to another to see what's going to happen next . . . I don't know what kind of characters my plays will

have until they . . . well, until they ARE . . . I don't conceptualise in any way.
Once I've got the clues I follow them – that's my job . . . to follow the clues.

In Act 1 of *The Caretaker*, we meet – briefly – the leather-jacketed Mick. When he hears voices, he leaves. The voices are those of Aston and Davies, a tramp. Aston offers hospitality to Davies, and unforced friendship. Davies is a demanding guest; nevertheless, Aston gives him a key, and leaves him in charge. Mick returns just as Davies is conducting a search of the premises. Act 2 finds Mick (Aston's brother) baiting Davies, hectoring him, making friendly overtures, and then teasing him, before leaving him once again, in Aston's care. Aston offers to take Davies on as caretaker. There is a further scene in which Mick bullies and befriends Davies by turns, before Aston (on the following morning) confides to Davies the secrets of his past and hoped-for future.

The curtain rises for Act 3 on Mick and Davies. The latter is complaining about Aston, and about the inhospitable treatment he has received. Two weeks have passed: two weeks in which Aston and Davies have been alone together. Mick is lying on the floor with his head on a roll of carpet, staring at the ceiling:

> DAVIES. *He's got no feelings!*
> Pause
> *See, what I need is a clock! I need a clock to tell the time! How can I tell the time without a clock? I can't do it! I said to him, I said, look here, what about getting in a clock, so's I can tell what time it is? I mean, if you can't tell what time you're at you don't know where you are, you understand my meaning? See, what I got to do now, if I'm walking about outside, I got to get my eye on a clock, and keep the time in my head for when I come in. But that's no good, I mean I'm not in here five minutes and I forgotten it. I forgotten what time it was!*
> DAVIES *walks up and down the room.*
> *Look at it this way. If I don't feel well I have a bit of a lay down, then, when I wake up, I don't know what time it is to go and have a cup of tea! You see, it's not so bad when I'm coming in. I can see the clock on the corner, the moment I'm stepping into the house I know what the time is, but when I'm in! It's when I'm in . . . that I haven't the foggiest idea what time it is!*
> Pause.
> *No, what I need is a clock in here, in this room, and then I stand a bit of a chance. But he don't give me one.*
> DAVIES *sits in the chair.*
> *He wakes me up! He wakes me up in the middle of the night! Tells me I'm making noises! I tell you I've half a mind to give him a mouthful one of these days.*

MICK.   *He don't let you sleep?*
DAVIES.   *He don't let me sleep! He wakes me up!*
MICK.   *That's terrible.*

Methuen edition, p 62

There are several clues in this scene as to things that might have been said in the course of the two weeks: Davies had asked for a knife and here he asks for a clock, and stops short of giving Aston a mouthful when Aston wakes him up and accuses him of making noises.

You could write a short scene, in which Davies does most of the talking, to bridge the gap between Acts 2 and 3.

Since this would be a creative assignment, you would need to justify your matter and manner of writing. In so doing, you would say much about the two characters and the conflict between them – and you would say much about the play's dramatic ideas – in a genuinely 'critical' way.

---

2 The significance of a title

It matters quite a lot what a novel, or play, or poem is called. It is not merely that one title is 'catchy', and another forgettable; a title is important because it tells us a lot about the author's intention, 'message' or predominating idea. Much of a work's character is captured in its name.

When we name a child, we confer an identity upon it. The child may not like the name, and so may change it – from Jonathan, say, to Jo, or from Katherine to Kate. In so doing, he or she spurns the identity conferred by parents and chooses a new one.

Writers not infrequently change the titles of their works. Jane Austen wrote a novel called *First Impressions*. She wrote it at a time when 'love at first sight' was the stock-in-trade of the sentimental novel. Austen's novel was about a heroine, Elizabeth Bennet, who fell in hate at first sight with the tall dark stranger, Darcy. When novels of the time were not being sentimental, they were moralising. *Pride and Prejudice*, as the novel was re-named, is 'about' not trusting to appearances – about swallowing the pride of prejudice, on the part of both Elizabeth and Darcy.

George Orwell (who had long discarded the identity locked up in his baptismal Eric Blair) thought to call his 1948 novel: *The Last Man in Europe*. It is an intriguing question whether the novel would have been as well known as it is if he had not thought again and called it: *Nineteen Eighty-Four*.

The playwright Arthur Miller knew how much there was in a name: he was married to a girl whose name (as they say) was a legend in her short lifetime. *Death of a Salesman* (1949) was Miller's second big play. He said of it:

> I have worked in two veins and I guess they alternate. In one, the event is inside the brain, and in the other, the brain is inside the event. In *Death of a Salesman*, we are inside the head.
>
> In *Arthur Miller*, by Ronald Hayman

The play is about the decline and fall of a Brooklyn salesman who drives himself to destruction in a dream of big sales and popularity. He quarrels with his boss – not because he is a quarrelsome man, but because he has tried to be something he is not. He has failed, and he has passed on his failure to his sons. The play psychoanalyses Willy Loman.

Arthur Miller had worked for his father, and had known salesmen. He had seen how they were treated by buyers in the big stores. The idea came to him of one such salesman, living in a frame-house that had once stood in open fields and reverberated to the shouts of boys. Now the house was overlooked by tall buildings and was empty. The boys had seen through their father and had gone; and the father, confronted by his own emptiness, had committed suicide. It was a powerful image: the house, the man's face, his mind at the end of its tether – unwinding before our eyes.

The play was tentatively called *The Inside of His Head*. Says the critic Benjamin Nelson: 'The play was to sweep outward from the mind of the salesman.' Every flashback was to take us deeper and deeper into Willy's consciousness, until he knew – and was known. His son Biff says at the end to his young brother Happy:

> BIFF. *He had the wrong dreams. All, all wrong.*
> HAPPY (almost ready to fight BIFF). *Don't say that!*
> BIFF. *He never knew who he was.*
>
> Penguin edition, pp. 110–11

We know something of who he was by the end of the play, because we have seen inside his head.

 You could say why you think Arthur Miller should have remained faithful to his original idea, embodied in the tentative title.

Or you could say why you think *Death of a Salesman* is the more appropriate title.

Is a title a sort of interpretation – a short-hand critique?

Or is it just packaging, that a play could do without? Come to that, is there any significance in the names Arthur Miller gave the characters in this play?

3 Interview with an actor

Actors are not best known for writing books about acting their parts (Simon Callow and Antony Sher – whom we shall meet in Chapter 4 – are exceptions), though they do sometimes talk to journalists. For the most part, we are left to guess at the difficulties they have had prior to the polished performance.

There are parts that present especial difficulties – and not a few of them are in the plays of Shakespeare. Obviously, the big parts – Lear, Macbeth, Othello, Antony, Hamlet and so on – can be played in a number of different ways, and have been. But where certain parts are concerned, one wonders how they can be played at all.

The part of the the Duke in *Measure for Measure* is one, rather notorious, example. A reviewer of a Royal Shakespeare Theatre production, in Stratford, had this to say:

> A moment's examination of the plot reveals the Duke as a rotten administrator, a lousy judge of character, and a weak and vain executive ducking the responsibility of enforcing his own laws. Yet, his muddling and meddling, for all the outrageous moral contradictions, will result – this is, just, a comedy – in the reassertion of a *human* justice, apparently as yielding as a flexicurve, but ultimately immutable and *good*.
>
> **Jill Burrows,**
> *The Times Educational Supplement,*
> 28 October 1983

To be both 'rotten', 'lousy', 'weak and vain' *and* 'immutable and good' makes heavy demands on an actor's skill.

The Duke, ruler of Vienna, leaves the state in the hands of his deputy, Angelo, on the pretence that he is going on a journey. In reality, he dons a friar's habit, and spies on his substitute and on his subjects. It is made known to him that the noble Claudio has enjoyed the favours of Juliet before their marriage. Under his own, lenient administration, Claudio might have suffered no more than a wigging, but Angelo is a harsher judge. In the new, moral Vienna, fornication is a capital offence.

The Duke admits that he had been too permissive:

> DUKE. We have strict statutes and most biting laws,
> The needful bits and curbs to headstrong weeds,
> Which for this fourteen years we have let slip
> . . . .
> . . . *in time the rod*

> *Becomes more mocked than feared, so our decrees,*
> *Dead to infliction, to themselves are dead,*
> *And liberty plucks justice by the nose;*
> *The baby beats the nurse, and quite athwart*
> *Goes all decorum.*
>
> (Act I, Scene iii)

He has left it to Angelo to restore order and discipline; therefore, when he visits Claudio and Juliet (separately) in their prison cells, he offers them very cold comfort indeed. To Juliet, first, he says:

> DUKE. *Love you the man that wronged you?*
> JULIET. *Yes, as I love the woman that wronged him.*
> DUKE. *So then it seems your most offenceful act*
>   *Was mutually committed?*
> JULIET.   *Mutually.*
> DUKE. *Then was your sin of heavier kind than his.*
> JULIET. *I do confess it, and repent it, father.*
>   . . . .
> DUKE.   *There rest.*
>   *Your partner, as I hear, must die tomorrow,*
>   *And I am going with instruction to him.*
>
> (Act II, Scene iii)

The instruction that he gives him is the famous:

> DUKE. *Be absolute for death: either death or life*
>   *Shall thereby be the sweeter. Reason thus with life:*
>   *If I do lose thee, I do lose a thing*
>   *That none but fools would keep . . .*
>
> (Act III, Scene i)

Claudio is a big enough fool to want to keep his life, as most of us are. That the worldly man should assume an ascetic's habit to preach resignation smacks of hypocrisy. This is certainly the view of the critic Michael Long. He says of the speech in Act III, Scene i, in which the Duke prefers death to life:

> The speech has often been seen as containing a severe but poignantly admirable Christian-stoic wisdom, but it looks to me like a continuation of Shakespeare's psychological portrait of this cold, petty, and frightened man.
>
> *The Unnatural Scene*, p. 83

Angelo does not only condemn two innocents to death, he adds insult to injury by attempting to seduce the novice nun Isabella, Claudio's sister, who had tried to intercede with him to spare her brother's life. This is the man who had broken his promise to his betrothed, Mariana, because her dowry had been lost at sea. And this is the man in whose hands the Duke had – 'with leavened and prepared choice' – placed the destinies of his subjects.

Of course, at the end of the play, the Duke rescues Isabella from Angelo, Claudio from the executioner, and Mariana from her 'moated grange'. He proves himself a wise judge, and his justice is poetic. This is, after all, 'just' a comedy.

Michael Long does not agree. The Duke, he says:

> Works his way steadily through the play to the last grotesque scene, where all his fantasies come true in a rush of manipulations and lever-pullings.
>   It is ghastly; but there have been many readers of the play who have not found it so. They have found the Duke admirable.
>
> (p. 84)

 Which sort of reader are you?

Neither reading is absolute. It is for the actor (and producer) to decide how the Duke should be played.

You could interview an (imaginary) actor taking the part of the Duke and ask him how he will play the part, and – in particular – how he will reconcile the 'lousy judge of character' with the 'immutable and good' judge of the final scene.

Or, more simply, you could say how you think the Duke would have to be played in order to be a credible figure – even a likeable one.

---

4 A first-night review

Sir Politic Would-Be (in Ben Jonson's *Volpone*) is another 'hard part to make sense of', according the *TES* drama critic Michael Church. The director Barry Russell seems to have agreed with him: in his Coventry production (see opposite) he cut Sir Politic and Lady Would-Be out of the play altogether.

When Bill Alexander directed the play at The Other Place in Stratford, the action lasted three and three-quarter hours. By making extensive cuts for showing to schools, Barry Russell trimmed the play down to only two hours. Ken Morley compromised: he did not savage the play, but he did prune it to make it more accessible to an audience accustomed to watching television.

Jill Burrows reviewed *Measure for Measure* and (Bill Alexander's) *Volpone* in the same article ('Twin Odysseys'). Having spoken of the moral ambiguities in the Shakespeare, she says:

Volpone is also in the business of juggling with moral perceptions. As with *Macbeth* and *Richard III*, we coast along with the bad guys until they go *too* far and we hotfoot back across the ethical divide and smugly enjoy the come-uppance of our surrogates.

Bill Alexander's production is consistently inventive and enjoyable. (At nearly four hours, it has to be.) Richard Griffiths's fox exerts a gap-toothed charm, earning our sympathy by patently glorying 'more in the cunning purchase ... than the glad possession' of his wealth and finding the laughs by playing straight down the line, slowly, firmly and truly.

The show is packed with excellent performances, rooted, in Jonsonian fashion, in a single desire. John Dicks (Corvino) brings an equally haggard obsessiveness to immuring and procuring his wife; James Fleet (Peregrine), by embroiling the audience in his own amazed disbelief at Sir Politic, succeeds in making the straight man funny, and Henry Goodman, with his Voltore, adds another accomplished creation to an already versatile season.

Jill Burrows

The Times Educational Supplement,
28 October 1983

Well said

Volpone.
Educational Theatre Projects, Whitefriars Museum and Gallery, Coventry.

A simple wooden platform, set in the centre of the long, timbered gallery of the 14th-century Whitefriars building, contains a bed and small table, while a natural embrasure in the wall, at one side of the stage, is hung with velvet curtains which hide Volpone's treasure. Such simple staging (appropriate for the schools tour which the company undertake at the end of January) throws the audience's attention on to the actors and the text; a text slimmed down to two hours playing time.

This gives the play, under Barry Russell's direction, a strong, propulsive drive, strengthening the narrative of the main plot and highlighting the theme of greed and its corrosive power. But it also robs it of its variety of texture (particularly in the absence of Sir Politic and Lady Would-Be). There is less comedy, and less light and shade generally in this production than can be found in the play.

In compensation, the language is well handled: long, convoluted, Jonsonian phrases clearly interpreted by the actors, details of character carefully shaded in as the plot develops and every twist of trickery sharply delineated.

Ann FitzGerald

The Times Educational Supplement

Alternative English

Way back when?

Volpone. By Ben Jonson. Half Moon Theatre.
When Did You Last See Your ... Trousers? By Ray Galton and John Antrobus. Garrick Theatre.

Volpone? But we all know *Volpone*. We've studied it, seen school productions of it, possibly acted in it ... Ben Jonson's comedy of manners basks in the sort of cosily unthinking familiarity which obscures the fact that it is, despite its formal perfection, a formidably difficult play for television-age audiences to grasp.

They can 'understand' it, in the sense of perceiving its simple moral point: greed blinds and debases. They can comprehend its intricately interlocking sub-plots. But their literary ear will have been attuned to the pared-down functionality of a very different kind of drama, whether on screen or stage: the profligate wit and the welter of classical and contemporary allusions put this play further out of reach than much of Shakespeare.

Behind this new version, which premiered last year at Birmingham Rep, there clearly lurks a sense of this uncomfortable truth. Ken Morley has pruned jokes, speeches, and even sub-plots in a valiant effort at accessibility, and has transposed the events from 1607 to an uneasily established 1977 (or thereabouts).

Morley himself plays Volpone, at once dainty and athletic, fastidious and gross; John Matshikiza plays his servant and accomplice Mosca with corresponding verve. This Mosca is black, and this master drools over him like a libidinous sugar-daddy: the relationship is richly comic, and has savage bite.

But the bite they put on their fellow-citizens is unfortunately far from lethal, and much of the blame for this must lie in slap-happy direction. Voltore (Tim Stern) glitters with greed, but neither of the other victims is delineated with the requisite vicious precision: Sir Politic Would-Be, admittedly a hard part to make sense of, fails to spark as a tweedy provincial; the episode in which he fails to conceal himself in a giant tortoise-shell was mistakenly made much of, and met with embarrassed silence.

Michael Church
The Times Educational Supplement

STRATFORD

Michael Billington

Volpone

BEN JONSON was always fascinated by the inordinate. And Bill Alexander's shrewd, intelligent production of Volpone at Stratford's Other Place recognises that Jonson's satirical bile is directed less against the posturing magnifico and his parasite than against the vicious predators who come to pluck at his carcase. At three-and-three-quarter hours, it is almost too much of a good thing; but it gets the moral balance of the play exactly right.

The key metaphor of the evening is acting. Richard Griffiths's splendid Volpone is, literally, a laid-back grandee who gets a big kick out of impersonation. At the first hint of a visitor, he whips out his make-up box, speckles his face with skin-rash, dons a sleazy gown and fox-fur and lets his right hand go feebly palsied. He is as much in

Richard Griffiths in Volpone

love with private theatricals as with gold. His four-square bed (with hidden drawers for quick-costume changes) becomes a stage as his dwarf, eunuch and hermaphrodite put on a show while he smokes a hookah; and he visibly swells with pride when he tells the hapless Celia 'I acted young Antinous and attracted the eyes and ears of all the ladies present.'

Volpone here becomes a closet ham who almost gets away with it and Mosca (deftly played by Miles Anderson) a working-class, black-leather boy rather more interested in the loot hidden behind the wooden panels of Alison Chitty's set. Not only does this distinguish between the two characters and highlight Jonson's delight in the mechanics of trickery: it also shows that the lawyer, merchant and old dotard who will go to almost any lengths to get Volpone's hoard are the real villains of the piece. I have seen them played as masked birds and comic cutouts. Here they become bourgeois Venetian monsters; and none more so than John Dick's stubbly, haunted Corvino who drags his wife towards Volpone's bed like a brutal cop manhandling a sit-down protester. Like all good satire, it is deeply shocking; and the effect is here compounded by the way Volpone and Mosca sit looking on with smug superiority.

The Guardian, 28 October 1983

'Like all good satire, it is deeply shocking.' Billington is not referring here merely to the fact that in parts of the play it is as bawdy as any Restoration comedy. There is such low comedy in *Measure for Measure*, involving Elbow, Froth and Mistress Overdone; but the opportunity (at least) for earthy word and gesture-play is much greater in *Volpone*. It may be imagined how much the earthlings, hot from taverns, must have roared, and how much the ladies (if any were present) must have blushed, or otherwise feigned deep shock.

But greed, dissoluteness and exploitation are the objects of quite as much fun and abuse as sensual debauch.

The jealous Corvino thinks to do Volpone (and therefore himself) a favour by granting him the loan of his virtuous wife. When Celia refuses to do Corvino's bidding, he threatens her in still more intemperate language than he had used before to lock her fast indoors. Celia protests that she would rather take poison than lie with Volpone.

> CORVINO.   Be damned!
> *Heart, I will drag thee hence, home, by the hair;*
> *Cry thee a strumpet, through the streets; rip up*
> *Thy mouth, unto thine ears; and slit thy nose,*
> *Like a raw rotchet – Do not tempt me, come.*
> *Yield, I am loath – Death, I will buy some slave,*
> *Whom I will kill, and bind thee to him, alive;*
> *And at my window, hang you forth: devising*
> *Some monstrous crime, which I, in capital letters,*
> *Will eat into thy flesh, with aquafortis,*
> *And burning corsives, on this stubborn breast.*
> *Now, by the blood, thou hast incensed, I'll do it.*
>
> (Act III, Scene vii)

What would the audience of 1605 have made of such verbal violence? What do we make of it now?

 You could put yourself in the position of a reviewer, shocked (or not) by the vices paraded before you on stage. You could write a review (perhaps in the style of one of the above), either as if you were at its very first night or at the première of a modern production.

Alternatively, you could compare the three productions reviewed above and, on the basis of your own close knowledge of the play, say what sort of production you would favour, and why.

---

5 Radio to stage

> *Under Milk Wood was first broadcast by the BBC on 25 January 1954. It was presented on the stage in the tenth Edinburgh Festival in 1956 and extracts from it were shown on BBC television. The stage production, by Douglas Cleverdon and Edward Burnham, of the play was given at the New (now Albury) Theatre, London, in 1956. The film of the play, which opened the Venice Festival in 1971, was released in 1972 with screenplay by Andrew Sinclair and starring Richard Burton and Peter O'Toole.*
>
> Dent, Everyman's Library edition, 1977

These words preface the Dent (Everyman's Library) edition of the play, published in 1977.

The work grew out of a broadcast talk, 'Quite Early One Morning' (1945), but Dylan Thomas was unsure whether the outgrowth should be a radio play, a verse-comedy, or a stage play. His final decision was that it should be 'a play for voices', and as such, it was first broadcast in its present form on 25 January 1954. There was still uncertainty about whether it was prose or verse: Thomas himself called it 'prose with blood-pressure'.

Thomas could not stop others calling it a verse-play; nor could he stop (because he was very dead) film-directors filming it, and play-producers adapting it for the stage. It has been read on public stages, in numerous languages; I have even seen it acted by a company of two – Sylvia Read and William Fry of Theatre Roundabout acting all 41 speaking parts – in a *tour de force* of memory and versatility that Thomas would have been the first to applaud.

There are problems in adapting this 'play for voices' for the stage, however. And not the least of them is that the action darts, like a hand-held torch, from one scene and one conversation to another. The torch is shone by the 'First Voice' and 'Second Voice'. The rapid flick from image to image is not a problem on radio, and it is the very meat and drink of film. But dialogue like the following would present problems on stage:

> SECOND VOICE.
>   *Evans the Death presses hard with black gloves on the coffin of his breast in case his heart jumps out.*
> EVANS THE DEATH (Harshly).
>   *Where's your dignity. Lie down.*

SECOND VOICE.

> Spring stirs Gossamer Beynon schoolmistress like a spoon.

GOSSAMER BEYNON (Tearfully).

> Oh, what can I do? I'll never be refined if I twitch.

SECOND VOICE.

> Spring this strong morning foams in a flame in Jack Black as he cobbles a high-heeled shoe for Mrs Dai Bread Two the gypsy, but he hammers it sternly out.

JACK BLACK (To a hammer rhythm).

> There is no leg belonging to the foot that belongs to this shoe.

SECOND VOICE.

> The sun and the green breeze ship Captain Cat sea-memory again.

CAPTAIN CAT.

> No, I'll take the mulatto, by God, who's captain here? Parlez-vous jig jig, Madam?

SECOND VOICE.

> Mary Ann Sailors says very softly to herself as she looks out at Llareggub Hill from the bedroom where she was born.

MARY ANN SAILORS (Loudly).

> It is Spring in Llareggub in the sun in my old age, and this is the Chosen Land.
> (A choir of children's voices suddenly cries out on one, high, glad, long sighing note)

> > Dent, Everyman's Library edition, pp. 50–1

One could omit lines (but that would be a shame); one could re-allocate them. (There is much to be said for dispensing with the First and Second Voices on stage. They might somehow be incorporated into the drama and be characters in their own right, conversing with each other. Robert Bolt did not give his narrator anywhere near as many lines. Alternatively, they could be 'voices over'.) One need change little. But *Under Milk Wood* is a verse-comedy, so as long as one is true to Thomas's 'idea', one might take liberties.

 You could either adapt part of *Under Milk Wood* (or other radio play – Tom Stoppard's *Albert's Bridge* would be an excellent candidate) for the stage, explaining fully what changes you have made and why.

Or you could say why you think Thomas's play is a radio play, and nothing but a radio play, or indeed whether you think *Under Milk Wood* lends itself to filming – for the big or the small screen.

6 A comparison

Measure for Measure is numbered among Shakespeare's comedies. *Volpone* is bawdy, black comedy. We have referred to Thomas's *Under Milk Wood* as comedy. But what is comedy?

Laughter there must be, that much is certain. *Measure for Measure* is *comédie* (drama) played by *comédiens* and *comédiennes* (actors), but its equivalent today would not be called 'comedy' because we do not find it funny. We call comedy – as in 'sitcom' (or situation comedy) – what we laugh at. We tend to think of the *comic* as the opposite of the *serious*.

The Importance of Being Earnest, by Oscar Wilde, is situation comedy at its most brilliant. Every other line provokes a smile, a chuckle, or outright laughter. There is scarcely one serious line from the beginning to the end of the play. 'Agricultural depression' is, of course, a very serious matter; but these portentous words are just another laugh-line in this exchange of barbs between Cecily and Gwendolen:

> GWENDOLEN (looking round). *Quite a well-kept garden this is, Miss Cardew.*
> CECILY. *So glad you like it, Miss Fairfax.*
> GWENDOLEN. *I had no idea there were any flowers in the country.*
> CECILY. *Oh, flowers are as common here, Miss Fairfax, as people are in London.*
> GWENDOLEN. *Personally I cannot understand how anybody manages to exist in the country, if anybody who is anybody does. The country always bores me to death.*
> CECILY. *Ah! This is what the newspapers call agricultural depression, is it not? I believe the aristocracy are suffering very much from it just at present. It is almost an epidemic amongst them, I have been told. May I offer you some tea, Miss Fairfax?*
> GWENDOLEN (with elaborate politeness). *Thank you.* (Aside) *Detestable girl. But I require tea!*
> CECILY (sweetly). *Sugar?*
> GWENDOLEN (superciliously). *No, thank you. Sugar is not fashionable any more.*
>   (CECILY *looks angrily at her, takes up the tongs and puts four lumps of sugar into the cup*)

Methuen Student Edition, p. 49

We have puns ('common', 'depression'), we have sarcasm (the 'lowest form of wit') and we have slapstick. But it is Algernon who has all the best lines, and the highest wit: 'Relations are simply a tedious pack of people, who haven't got the remotest knowledge of how to live, nor the smallest instinct about when to die'; 'All women become like their mothers. That is their tragedy. No man does. That's his.' This is comedy-as-fun at its economic best.

But there is more to comedy than fun – certainly to much modern comedy. There is a very sharp edge indeed to Mike Harding's 'political' comedy, for example. It's an edge sharpened on anger. He has said:

> I've always been political. I think I was born left-wing (...) There's no room in my mind any more for people who are fence-sitters – you're either for us or against us (...) The alienation of an audience is everything to a good comedian, you have to risk it. What do you want me to do – push the safe buttons? Irish jokes, Paki jokes, jokes against women?
>
> *The Guardian*, 1987

A show by the 'alternative' comedian Gerry Sadowitz was called Total Abuse. He boasts that he's the world's most offensive comedian. He joked about the Hungerford Massacre:

> I blame the victims. They shouldn't have left home without their American Express Cards.
>
> *The Guardian*, 1987

And he says of himself, using the same word as Mike Harding used:

> Life to me is academic. I feel like an alien from another planet.
>
> *The Guardian*, 1987

Alexei Sayle is another comedian who thrives on alienation and on outraging his audience. He said to Ian Williams of the *Independent*:

> My big contribution to stand-up comedy was that I reckon I was the first performer who genuinely didn't care what the audience thought. Most comics, even the insulting ones, can't go far enough because they still want to be loved by their audience.
>
> *The Independent*, 1987

Comedians, by Trevor Griffiths, is a play about stand-up comedy. Eddie Waters is a comic of the old school of the northern clubs. He used to be called the 'Lancashire Lad'. Now he runs an evening class for trainee comedians. In a 1987 production of this 1975 play at the Young Vic, the part of Eddie Waters was taken by Bert Parnaby, himself an ex-teacher of drama. Willie Ross played the Club Secretary, or compère, at the club at which Eddie's trainees make their début and hope to catch the eye of a visiting talent-scout.

BERT PARNABY

WILLIE ROSS

For thirteen years Bert Parnaby was a teacher in Manchester and, like Eddie Waters, used to give evening classes there. For a good part of his working life Bert Parnaby was Her Majesty's Inspector of Schools for Drama, particularly in the Greater London area, though in the fifties he was a radio producer in the BBC North region. In 1980 he followed his son Alan into the acting profession, making his debut at the Theatre Royal, Stratford East in *This Jockey Drives Late Nights*. After a Falstaff at the Belgrade, Coventry, and a season with the RSC, he worked exclusively in television. Recent credits include *On the Palm* and *Faces of Cromwell* in *Timewatch* (BBC); *First Among Equals* (Granada) and *The Bretts* (Central). His first film role was as the magistrate in *Prick Up Your Ears*.

Willie Ross has spent the last eighteen years working as the comedy half of one of the country's best comedy double acts. He started in the Northern Clubs and has worked with some of the top names in variety theatre including Les Dawson, Roy Hudd, Michael Barrymore, John Junkin, The Krankies and finally Des O'Connor and Paul Nicholas at the London Palladium. Since going solo, he has appeared in the films *Rita, Sue and Bob Too* and *The Fear*, Franco Rosso's *Nature of the Beast, Road* for the BBC and most recently in Jim Henson's *The Storyteller* starring John Hurt.

From the programme of The Young Vic production *Comedians* by Trevor Griffiths

Comedians is about these men and their world. But into this world irrupts a young man with the Harding–Sadowitz–Sayle 'alternative' philosophy of comedy. Gethin Price has no time for the Eddie Waters routine. His comedy issues from pure hate.

> PRICE (to himself, not admitting the audience's existence). *Wish I had a train. I feel like smashing a train up. On me own. I feel really strong. Wish I had a train. I could do with some exercise.*

(He does a complicated kata, with praying mantis footsweeps, a tan-fui, pa-kua dao, and other Kung Fu exercises. A spot suddenly illuminates larger than life-size dummies of a youngish man and woman carried on by a club-hand. Well dressed, beautiful people, a faint unselfconscious arrogance in their carriage. The man wears evening dress, gloves, etc, the girl, a simple, stunning white full-length dress and wrap. Her arm is looped in his. They stand, perhaps waiting for a cab to show after the theatre. PRICE has continued his exercises throughout this 'arrival'. Becomes aware of them gradually: rises slowly: stares. Turns to the audience, slowly smiles, evil and childlike. Sniffs. Ambles over. Stands by the man, measuring, walks round to stand by the girl. We sense him being ignored. He begins to inspect the girl minutely. Takes a cigarette from pocket.) *Cigarette?* (Nothing. He offers it to the man.) *No?* (He pockets the cigarette, turns, calls 'Taxi!' sharply out front, shakes his head as it disappears. Moves round the man's side again.) *Are you the interpreter, then? Been to the match, have we? Were you at t'top end wi' lads? Good, wannit? D'you see Macari? Eh? Eh?* (Silence) *P'raps I'm not here. Don't you like me? You hardly know me. Let's go and have a pint, get to know each other. Here, don't you live in Salford? I swear I've seen you at the dog track.* (Nothing. He takes a cigarette out of the man's top pocket.) *Very kind of you. Ta.* (He lights the cigarette, blows the smoke in slow separate puffs across the man's face.) *Int this nice? I like a good chat.* (Intimate, man-to-man.) *Eh. I bet she's a goer, int she, sunshine? She's got a fair pair of knockers on her too.*

Faber edition, p. 49

You could compare *The Importance of Being Earnest* with *Comedians*, focusing on the nature of the comedy in the two plays.

Or you could compare the three attitudes towards (or 'philosophies' of) comedy expressed in the words and actions of Gethin Price, Eddie Waters and Bert Challenor, the talent scout from the 'big time'. With which point of view do you find yourself in most sympathy, and why? Does Griffiths himself appear to identify with the view of any one of these three comedians?

7 Novelisation

Films are always being based on novels – many have already been referred to in these pages. Films have been made of plays, and plays have been made of novels. Films, in their turn, have been 'novelised' – but plays seem to have escaped this treatment (if we except all the narrative versions of the plays of Shakespeare that there have been).

There is a sense, though, in which a novelist (or story-writer) can tell us more about a character than a playwright can. In a play, we learn about characters from what they say, from what they do, and from what other characters say about them. In a novel, we can learn still more about them from what they *think* (or from what the novelist chooses to tell us they think). As Golding put it (see page 5) we can

> ... thread in and out of a single mind and body, (and) so live another life.

A novel or short story, then, affords us a degree of intimacy with a character (or characters) that we do not have in a play, even when an actor plays that character in such a way as to move us to tears or laughter, and enlist our sympathy for – even conjure identity with – that character.

Wole Soyinka was the first African – indeed, he was the first black writer – to win the Nobel Prize for Literature, in 1986. He had by then published 20 books of plays, poetry and fiction. Soyinka is a story-teller in a long West African tradition. His plays are stories, therefore they lend themselves to rendering as narrative fiction.

Throughout his work there runs a loathing of oppression, whether it is that of the white supremacist or the corrupt black politician. *Camwood on the Leaves* was written (like *Under Milk Wood*) for radio, and was first broadcast by the BBC in London in 1965. It tells the story of teenage lovers, Isola and Morounke. Isola has made Morounke pregnant and incurred the wrath of his father, Reverend Erinjobi. Erinjobi (who is this play's oppressor) has made an outcast of Isola. The boy and girl return to a childhood haunt in the forest. They seek to be far away from their parents, but they are truly haunted by Erinjobi, the name Isola has given to a marauding boa. Isola keeps a gun to kill the snake – but it isn't the snake that he kills.

In the following extract, Isola and Morounke reflect on their escape:

ISOLA. *Come here, Morounke. Stand here ... here, under the light.*
MOROUNKE. *Why? Why do you look at me?*
ISOLA. *Do you feel different? You are a woman now, do you feel that?*
MOROUNKE. *I don't know.*
ISOLA. *Come nearer ... let me listen. That is where the child should be.*
(Pause) *There is no sound.*
MOROUNKE. *My mother was trying to listen too.*
ISOLA. *(furious) Don't ever let her do that again!*
MOROUNKE. *Why, Isola, what is the matter?*
ISOLA. *Sorry ... it's nothing ... nothing ...*
MOROUNKE. *You frightened me.*

ISOLA.   *I'm sorry. It's nothing... You say you want to stay here?*

MOROUNKE.   *I'm not going tonight. I haven't the strength to leave this place. I must stay with you.*

ISOLA.   *It is my child. You are almost a child yourself, do you know that?*

Pause

MOROUNKE.   *Isola.*

ISOLA.   *Yes.*

MOROUNKE.   *They are telling lies about you all over the town. Bimpe told me. They say you beat... your father. All over the town, they've been cursing you.*

ISOLA.   *And did I beat him?*

MOROUNKE.   *I don't know.*

ISOLA.   *But you were there, weren't you?*

MOROUNKE.   *I ran away. Your father frightened me, Isola. He was so terrible. When he picked up his walking-stick, I ran away. I was very frightened. I ran away to Bimpe.*

ISOLA.   *I ran away too. I remember he raised the stick against me and I took it from him and broke it. He tried to struggle for it. Then I went home. I still remember the crowd who had gathered together. They made way for me as if I was a leper. They shrank from me. I knew suddenly what it means to be an outcast. Before I reached home, my mother had somehow heard of it. She was wailing and beating her breast as if a great disaster had befallen the family. The children were huddled together. They were clinging to one another in terror.*

Methuen edition, pp. 106–7

 You could rewrite *Camwood on the Leaves* (or another of the *Six Plays*) as a short story. What would make this a critical piece of writing (rather than a piece of slavishness) would be the extent to which you rendered the dialogue (or most of it) as an account of the workings of the mind, or of the feelings, of the characters. You would be adding to the story that intimacy that is lacking in the play.

8 Programme notes

What does one expect to see in a theatre programme? A programme is not an advertisement for the play because the consumers have bought the product already. Nor is it a review of the play, though the management may well want to quote from favourable reviews of earlier performances:

> Entertaining from first to last.
>
> *The Independent*

> You'll have to run to catch up with this one.
> *Daily Mail*
>
> A masterpiece of spell-binding showmanship.
> *The Times*

Playgoers will certainly want to know who is in the play, who directed it, and who stage-managed it. They may also be interested in who was responsible for lighting, music, costumes and any fight sequences or dancing that there might be. All this information is given on the title page inside the programme, such as the one for Tom Stoppard's *Jumpers* at the Aldwych Theatre, London (below). 'Movement', credited to David Toguri, included some quite demanding gymnastics. In The Young Vic *Comedians* programme, there were credits to Dave Lee for Kung Fu instruction and to Perry Montague-Mason for violin lessons.

ALDWYCH THEATRE
ALDWYCH, LONDON, WC2
Box Office 01-836 6404   01-379 6233
Licensee: NEDERLANDER THEATRES (ALDWYCH) LIMITED
Chairman: JAMES M. NEDERLANDER
Under the Management of: MICHAEL CODRON LIMITED

MICHAEL CODRON
presents

PAUL EDDINGTON and **FELICITY KENDAL**

SIMON CADELL

in a new production of

TOM STOPPARD'S

JUMPERS

with

TIMOTHY BATESON

GAIL ROLFE

and

ANDREW SACHS

Directed by **PETER WOOD**
Designed by **CARL TOMS**
Lighting by **DAVID HERSEY**
Movement by **DAVID TOGURI**
Musical Supervision by CHRIS WALKER
Costumes by BRUCE SNYDER
Sound by AUTOGRAPH
Associate Producer **DAVID SUTTON**

From the programme of *Jumpers* by Tom Stoppard produced at the Aldwych Theatre, London

There is likely to be a photograph of each prominent actor, together, perhaps, with a brief thumbnail biography – as there was of Bert Parnaby and Willie Ross, among others (see page 52). There may also be biographies of the director and the designer, and a history of the company of which they are members.

Most programmes do say something about the play though – particularly when it is a play full of ideas. The small programme for the small-cast production of *Under Milk Wood* by Theatre Roundabout contained a 330-word account of the genesis of the play, and of the circumstances in which it was written. The *Comedians'* programme 'note' ran to more than 1,700 words – twice as many words as a student might expect to use in a coursework essay. Edward Braun, of the University of Bristol, quoted from Griffiths to explain how the idea for the play came to him, and he gave an account of the reception given to the play by theatre managements, reviewers and theatregoers. This is *not* the sort of thing a student would be expected to write about in a coursework essay.

But Braun goes on to talk about Gethin Price, and his 'angry, self-denying "hardness"'. Gethin is a philosopher in his ruthless, working-class way, and his philosophy of comedy is the play's dominating 'idea'.

The central character in *Jumpers* is a philosopher, too.

> ...the heart of the play lies in the lecture being hammered out by moral philosopher George Moore on the question of whether God exists and whether social morality is conditioned by environment or is the result of Divine law.
>
> Michael Billington in *The Guardian*

While Moore debates morals, his house (if not his system) accommodates murder and adultery. His wife is a one-time showbiz personality up to her cups in intrigue. Inspector Bones is an admirer, who calls to do his duty bearing flowers:

BONES. *Ah! – Bones!*
GEORGE. *What?*
BONES. *As in rags-and.*
GEORGE. *Rags and bones???*
BONES. *Yes – no. Bones' the name, as in dem bones, dem bones... (Pause)... dem dry bones. That's a tortoise is it.*
GEORGE. *I'm sorry, I was expecting a psychiatrist.*
BONES. *No really?*
   (BONES *is himself again, master of any situation. He advances past* GEORGE *on the last line.*)

GEORGE. I'm really rather busy.
  (BONES is now past him. BONES looks at GEORGE with unconcealed interest.)
BONES. What is it that you do?
GEORGE. I'm a professor of moral philosophy.
BONES (wagging a finger). I'm very glad that you said that, son.
  (BONES continues his inspection of the hall.)
GEORGE. Perhaps I can help you.
BONES. In my inquiries, you mean, or just generally? Think carefully before you answer – if it gets about that you're helping me in my inquiries, bang goes your credit at the off-licence for a start. Inspector Bones, C.I.D. – tell Miss Moore I'm here, there's a good lad.
GEORGE (rather coldly). It's Mrs Moore, actually.
BONES. Moore is her married name?
GEORGE. Yes, Moore is my name.
BONES (shrewdly). You are the husband.
GEORGE. Yes.
BONES. Professor . . . Moore.
GEORGE. Yes . . . (Lightening.) Yes, I'm something of a *logician* myself.
BONES. Really? Sawing ladies in half, that sort of thing?
GEORGE. Lo *gician*. (BONES is casing the hall expertly, just with his eyes.) Would you like me to take your flowers, Inspector?
BONES. I was hoping to see Miss Moore personally.
GEORGE. Well, it's awfully nice of you to come round . . .
BONES. Not at all. If I'm going to arrest her, I can hardly do it by Interflora.

Faber edition, p. 44–5

The humour is zany, surreal. The action is fast and flirtatious. An audience might be forgiven for wanting to read, in the interval or when the play is over, the considered opinion of what it was 'about' by someone who has read it and thought about it. Intelligent playgoers will not expect a definitive interpretation: they know there is no such thing; but they will want some drawing together of threads that may well hang loose in the torrent of images, and flashes of wit and nakedness of a stage production.

 You could write such a programme note. What features of the play would you want to draw attention to, to ensure that they are not missed? What would interest you about the play if you were seeing it for the first time? What ideas would you want to consider, and perhaps discuss later when the show is over?

THREE

Poems

What is a poem?

It is the mode of writing that students find most difficult – or least congenial – to talk or write about. This may be because:

1. Poetry is an unfamiliar sort of writing – one does not come across poems in the same way that one comes across plays on the television, or stories in magazines, or letters on one's mat.
2. Poets seem to speak a private sort of language from which the readers of novels and newspapers are excluded, and critics make matters worse by being solemn about poems, as if they were by definition high culture, like keyboard sonatas, beyond the reach of *hoi polloi*.

Having asked what is a novel and what is a play, the only safe answer to the question what is a poem would seem to be: a poem is whatever a poet or poetry publisher or critic says it is. This is certainly the view of the fifth of the five correspondents below who wrote to the editor of the *Guardian* in May 1987. A leader writer had remarked that there seemed to be 'a growing demand for poetry'. John Fraser of Leeds wrote in as follows:

Sir, — As your Leader of May 9 contends, there may well be a growing demand for poetry. But what sort of poetry?

Is the need for true verse and all the arts of poetry — as practised by Milton, Shakespeare, Keats, Wordsworth, Tennyson and Shelley, for instance — or do you refer to the chopped-up prose known as 'free' poetry, devoid of rhyme and rhythm, which masquerades as the real thing?

One is entitled to ask what has happened to the dictionary — and long-accepted — definition. Even in schools, youngsters are not being taught versification. Local newspapers contain examples of shattered prose written by children and based on themes and words fed to them by teachers.

Surely, poetry should strive to communicate; but much of today's writing is no doubt intended for the occult circle, which appears to mistake obscurity of meaning for profundity.

There is, I believe, a point beyond which some of this 'free' poetry becomes merely a sort of literary puzzle with little or none of the emotional content one finds in poems that have stood the test of time. My impression is that much of it is ephemeral and will be swept into obscurity by the passage of time.

It is true that poetry can dispense with rhyme — though it is likely to be the poorer for doing so — and Margaritae Sorori, by Henley, is a fine example. But if it lacks rhythm, how does it differ from prose?

You are right to refer to a renaissance, which means a return to real poetry. No wonder that Betjeman, who was a reasonably orthodox poet, was a best seller!

I believe that the evidence would show that what is wanted is poetry that is not too difficult to be understood by aesthetically minded and normally intelligent people and gives them real pleasure. Isn't it high time that the critics roused themselves and questioned the modern syndrome? Or are they tarred with the same brush?

Could it be another example of the Emperor's Clothes? — Yours hopefully.
John Fraser
10 The Drive,
Leeds.

The Guardian, 1987

Michael Howlett wrote from a mulberry bush, two days later, to defend free verse against Mr Fraser's nostalgia for the 'real poetry' of John Betjeman. Three days later still, Stephen Meyer spoke up for his fellow Leedsman, and for 'rhymed, formal verse':

Blank shots

Sir, — John Fraser whose own letter (May 13) ends with a reasonable alexandrine, laments the state of much that passes for modern poetry. He complains that the 'chopped-up prose known as "free" poetry' is devoid of rhyme and rhythm.

Does he really believe it is possible to think or write *without* rhythm? If so, could he give us a demonstration?

As for rhyme, it went out of fashion after the first world war. Along with innocence and the belief in progress, it died in the trenches.

Mr Fraser's longing for the certainties of iambic pentameters and lines rhyming alternately is an understandable nostalgia for an age that has gone. Surely 'aesthetically minded and normally intelligent people' will not be deluded into believing that simple rhymes and a nice, comforting metre will make everything all right again? — Yours faithfully,
Michael Howlett.
Mulberry Bush, Standlake, Oxfordshire.

Sir, — Michael Howlett's comment that 'Rhyme .. went out of fashion after the first world war' (Letters, May 15) is wrong but significant. There are acres of Wordsworth and whole barren fields of Walt Whitman before the First World War (I seem to recall a few other names: Milton, was it? Shakespeare, perhaps?), all with complete independence of rhyme. More recently, Eliot, Auden, e.e. cummings and Geoffrey Hill have used rhyme to great purpose.

The significance of what Mr Howlett says lies in the use of that word, 'fashion.' There is certainly a fashion today, particularly among poets who are not, as Geoffrey Hill has expressed it, 'obsessed with the recalcitrance of language,' to eschew the formal discipline of verse and see how far they can get away with it. Well, they've done very well up to now. But it is still, as Mr Howlett points out, a fashion, and fashions change.

The English language is peculiarly rich in words, and therefore in rhymes. Its loss of grammatical declension and the breadth and variety of its vocabulary make it particularly apt for rhymed, formal verse, and it is this, in spite of the best efforts of liberal teachers and self-publicists, which is what most of us still think of when we hear the word 'poetry.'

I recall the experience of a friend of mine, who was about to send some avant-garde verses to the Third Programme. He was on the point of posting them, when he reflected that payment was by the line. He re-wrote the pieces, chopping each line in half, and doubled his money. No wonder 'free' verse is popular! — Yours faithfully,
Stephen Meyer,
5 Waveney Road,
Leeds.

Sir,
Probably
The nearest thing to
A definition
Of poetry
Is that it is written
In lines: no attempt
Is made to make
A regular margin on
The right hand side:
Capitals mark the left
sometimes.
But strictly
All those things we call
Poems have nothing
In common except
That they are
All called
Poems. Probably.
   Yours,
J. Gillie.
15 North Road,
Southampton.

The Guardian, 1987

None of the above four writers contends that rhyme is necessary to a poem, though Messrs Fraser and Meyer evidently prefer rhymed verse. Perhaps rhyme does, indeed, pass into and out of fashion. Mr Howlett thinks it is out; Leeds thinks it is coming back. Mr Meyer does not counter Mr Howlett's point about rhythm, so it does appear to be conceded that writing – prose or poetry – is unthinkable *without* it.

Is there nothing about a poem that makes it a poem, and not a piece of 'shattered prose', apart from its being a poem because it is so called? Mr Fraser refers to the dictionary and to the 'long-accepted' definition of poetry to be found there – but he does not quote it. This is part of the Chambers definition of 'poem':

> **poem,** $\bar{po}'im$, *em, n.* a composition in verse: a composition of high beauty of thought or language and artistic form, typically, but not necessarily, in verse . . .
>
> *Chambers Twentieth Century Dictionary*

Beauty of some sort seems to be the main qualification. Of course, beauty is in the eye of the beholder. But it is to be wondered whether Mr Fraser would think 'Executive' by the 'reasonably orthodox' Betjeman, a thing of beauty. The first half of the poem goes like this:

> *I am a young executive. No cuffs than mine are cleaner;*
> *I have a Slimline brief-case and I use the firm's Cortina.*
> *In every roadside hostelry from here to Burgess Hill*
> *The* maîtres d'hotel *all know me well and let me sign the bill.*
>
> *You ask me what it is I do. Well actually, you know,*
> *I'm partly a liaison man and partly P.R.O.*
> *Essentially I integrate the current export drive*
> *And basically I'm viable from ten o'clock till five.*
>
> *For vital off-the-record work – that's talking transport-wise –*
> *I've a scarlet Aston Martin – and does she go? She flies!*
> *Pedestrians and dogs and cats – we mark them down for slaughter.*
> *I also own a speed-boat which has never touched the water.*
>
> From *A Nip in the Air,* John Murray, 1974

It is more likely that Betjeman strove for amusement than for beauty. He would have been the first to admit that 'Executive' is 'rhymed formal verse' (to quote Mr Meyer), not poetry at all.

A poem need not be in verse, then; and verse may well not be poetry. One could agree that prose at its best is a thing of 'high beauty of thought or language and artistic form'. I would contend that, by these criteria, Golding's novel *The Spire* and Arthur Miller's play *The Crucible* are poetry – and another contributor to the

Guardian correspondence above would agree with me. Michael Paffard of Keele, Staffordshire, attempted to distinguish between poetry and prose thus:

> ... In prose there is an understanding between the writer and reader that what is being said could be communicated in a different selection of language; in other words, it is paraphrasable.
>
> The less true this becomes the nearer the language is approaching poetry, which is inherently unparaphrasable without loss of meaning whether it is in verse or not. There is no clear *formal* dividing line and no absurdity in saying that many passages of prose are poetry...
>
> **Michael Paffard,**
> 3 Church Bank, Keele, Staffordshire.
>
> *The Guardian,* 1987

– but not, of course, vice versa. Poetry, by definition, cannot be prose.

According to Mr Paffard's definition of poetry then, it is perfectly acceptable to think of *The Spire, The Crucible,* Lawrence's *The White Stocking,* The Book of Job, and the prose dialogues in Shakespeare's plays as poetry. Miller once said, in fact:

> I've been writing verse for years, but primarily as an exercise, to contract and squeeze the language and clear the mind...

There is more poetry in almost any of the speeches in Miller's plays than in the likes of Betjeman's 'Executive' (splendid verse though it is).

Yet no short story, no play, no novel can be called a poem, in the sense in which we use this word in the twentieth century – and this chapter is about poems, not poetry. Part of the problem, where definition is concerned, is that the *function* of poetry has undergone so much change. Time was when poems and stories were one and the same thing, and when it was as natural for actors to speak in verse as it was for boys to play female parts. Nowadays, we expect stories and plays to be in prose, and we expect poems to be short.

Howard Sergeant was editor for 42 years of a poetry magazine called *Outposts*. He said once to the editor of the magazine *Words* that he received 1,600 poems every week from writers who hoped he would publish their work. Even if a lot of these poems were 'chopped-up prose', and still more were verse in 'Executive' style, that's still an awful lot of poems. Mercifully, most of them will have been short.

To return to the two reasons suggested at the beginning of this chapter for students' difficulties in this mode of writing, it would seem that poetry is *not* unfamiliar because plays and novels can be poetry and eighty-odd thousand poems drop on to one editor's mat in the course of a year – so *poems* are pretty familiar, too (to the point, perhaps, of editorial contempt).

It is not true to say either that (all) poems are private, solemn products of high culture. The above-mentioned editor of *Words* (now co-editor of *Words International*), Phillip Vine, reviewed Bob Dylan's *Lyrics 1962–1985*. He concluded his review with these words:

Bob Dylan

> When he takes himself seriously as a poet as in SOME OTHER KINDS OF SONGS (the sleeve notes for ANOTHER SIDE OF DYLAN) he can produce poetry – some of it rhyming – of the very highest quality:
>
> *high treachery sails*
> *unveils*
> *its last wedding song...*
>
> *the people've been set t' try t' forget*
> *that their*
> *whole life's a honeymoon*
> *over soon...*
>
> *clang sang the preacher*
> *inside of the altar*
> *outside of the theatre*
> *mystery fails*
> *when treachery prevails*
> *the forgotten rosary*
> *nails*
> *itself t' a cross*
> *of sand*
>
> *all is lost Cinderalla*
> *all is lost*

Words International, January 1988

Is a 'lyric' a poem? It is, if a reviewer says it is.

What do we look for in a poem?

From what has already been said, we must above all be looking for *poetry*. Poetry does not always come in the form of *poems*, but a poem must always be poetry, if it is not to be verse, or worse.

What is the poetry, then, that we shall look for in poems and that we sometimes find in pieces of writing that are not poems? The dictionary says it has to do with beauty. So what's beauty? Chambers (again) defines it as follows:

> **beauty,** *bū'ti, n.* the quality that gives pleasure to the sight, or aesthetic pleasure generally . . .

Beauty has to do with pleasure, then; something beautiful is something that is pleasing to the senses.

Many fine poems are beautiful in these terms – indeed, they are hymns to beauty:

A Town Window

Beyond my window in the night
   Is but a drab, inglorious street,
Yet there the frost and clean starlight
   As over Warwick woods are sweet.

Under the grey drift of the town
   The crocus works among the mould
As eagerly as those that crown
   The Warwick spring in flame and gold.

And when the tramway down the hill
   Across the cobbles moans and rings,
There is about my window-sill
   The tumult of a thousand wings.

John Drinkwater (1882–1937)

In just twelve lines, the poet evokes images that appeal to almost all our senses. But is poetry to be confined to pleasing and to appealing to our senses, and are poems to be hymns only and poets praise-singers?

W. H. Auden died in 1973. The writer of his unsigned obituary in *The Times* of 1 October said of (particularly his early) work that its 'simplicity of imagery and statement' persuaded one of 'his having something to say which was worth saying'.

'His next poems', the writer went on '("Spain 1937", for instance, or "In Praise of Limestone") have arguments, and these arguments, however brilliantly clothed in diction or metaphor, are of supreme importance.'

OBITUARY
W. H. AUDEN
The outstanding English poet of his generation

The Times, 1 October 1973

The obituary concluded with these words:

> ...we owe to him above all our sense that the greatest poetry must observe, absorb and criticize the public events and social conditions of its own time.

Diction and metaphor (and rhyme, and metre, and stanza-pattern) all add to poetry – but they are no more than the accidents of a poem; they are not essential to it. What is essential is the argument, the observation, the criticism – in a word: the idea. The Georgian John Drinkwater was a minor poet, because, in so far as his poems expressed ideas at all, these were not of 'supreme importance' in his work. His work was pleasing (even 'beautiful'), but it was not significant, because it did not address issues of significance.

Seamus Heaney makes this point in *The Government of the Tongue*, published in 1988. He compares the early work of Auden (and that of Wilfred Owen, Philip Larkin and Derek Walcott) with the poems of hundreds of minor talents, wrapped in 'genteel self-absorption'. Auden and company wrestled with the issues that troubled their times, as Drinkwater and company did not. I take Heaney's point: I believe a poem that is to be 'great' must grapple with subjects of some importance. No amount of literary finesse will make a poem great whose subject is trivial. But I take Andrew Motion's point, also (who reviewed Heaney's book for the *Independent*):

> Heaney has too intelligent a heart to argue that a precise correlation exists between a poem's subject and its quality, or that the grislier the subject the greater the merit.

One can argue, one can observe, one can criticise, one can express ideas, with a gentleness of touch, without bombast and high seriousness.

Poet David R. Morgan was writer-in-residence for some months at Fairfield Psychiatric Hospital in Hitchin, Hertfordshire. He wrote about the experience, and collected certain of the poems that patients had written in an article published in *Words International* (February 1988). One of these poems was a three-liner:

> *That's Rich*
>
> *It is easier for a camel*
> *To pass through the eye of a needle,*
> *If you put it in a liquidiser first.*
>
> Paul Daly

Morgan would not, Paul Daly would not, I would not say this is a great poem; but it *is* a poem. It is not the 'grisly' subject; it is not the arrangement of lines; it is not even the fact that Morgan calls it a poem that makes it a poem. It is a poem because it has a presiding idea. Rather, it has not one idea: it suggests several possible ideas. It provokes us to ideas. Its title, its distortion of the gospel aphorism and its comic-grotesque last line combine to raise questions. Arthur Miller wrote verse because it rubbed off on to his plays. He wanted his audience 'to feel that they're getting a packed, a dense speech'. And that is what we have come to look for in poems: a certain conciseness, tightness, tautness of language; lines that are, perhaps, unparaphrasable, to re-use Paffard's term; language strong enough to sustain multiple layers of meaning; ideas that spin like plates, and that keep them spinning.

As this last thought suggests, we also (still) do look for a figure of speech: a metaphor, at least one strong, sharply focused image. It will probably need to be original: a comparison that arrests the attention because it hasn't been made before, like Auden's comparison of Spain (in 'Spain') to a 'fragment nipped off from hot Africa, soldered so crudely to inventive Europe'. But the image need not be new: it might be an old one, re-worked. Lest it be thought that I would deny the title poet to John Betjeman, I shall give him this section's last word – one of his very last. 'The Last Laugh' has all that we look for in a poem.

The Last Laugh

I made hay while the sun shone.
    My work sold.
Now, if the harvest is over
    And the world cold,
Give me the bonus of laughter
    As I lose hold.

From *A Nip in the Air*,
John Murray, 1974

How might one write about a poem?

1 Poetry and politics

John Drinkwater, referred to above as a 'minor talent', was not a political poet. That is he did not question (or he did not question *as a poet*) the right to hold power of those who held it. Few of the poets of his day did. John Masefield, Walter de la Mare, James Elroy Flecker, Rupert Brooke, W. H. Davies and others contributed to a volume of *Georgian Poetry*, published in 1912. Their poetry was as solid, conservative and assured as the *Titanic* that went down in the same year.

W. H. Auden was a political poet, and – as we have seen – this was one reason why *The Times* called him the 'outstanding English poet of his generation'. This judgement has nothing to do with Auden's party affiliation; it has to do with his commitment to deeply held values, his concern for the human condition, and his espousal of causes. He never (well, hardly ever) wrote a trivial poem. He once wrote:

> even a limerick
> ought to be something a man of
> honour awaiting death from cancer
>   or a firing squad
> could read without contempt

R. S. Thomas is a political poet, too. He writes about Wales – but he does not write about Wales in the way that the Georgians wrote about England. He was born in English-speaking Cardiff in 1913. It was only when, as an adult, he became a country parson in mid-Wales that he learned Welsh in order to speak to his parishioners in their own tongue. He was always ambivalent in his attitude towards them: in poems like 'Evans', 'The Labourer' and 'Death of a Peasant', he both paid tribute to their long-suffering acceptance of hardship, and wondered at their almost animal simplicity. But, on balance, he respected Prytherch, his representative Welshman. He fought against a tendency to condescension in himself, and he told his English readers not to pity Prytherch:

> *... hold your tears*
> *For his name also is written in the Book of Life.*
>
> *Ransack your brainbox, pull out the drawers*
> *That rot in your heart's dust, and what have you*
> > *to give*
> *To enrich his spirit or the way he lives?*
>
> From 'Affinity'

That challenge of his reveals a certain impatience with outsiders – with tourists who came to Wales for their holiday because it was 'quaint'.

> *I saw them stare*
> *From their long cars, as I passed knee-deep*
> *In ewes and wethers. I saw them stand*
> *By the thorn hedges, watching me string*
> *The far flocks on a shrill whistle.*
>
> *And always there was their eyes' strong*
> *Pressure on me; You are Welsh, they said;*
> *Speak to us so; keep your fields free*
> *Of the smell of petrol, the loud roar*
> *Of hot tractors; we must have peace*
> *And quietness.*
> > *Is a museum*
> *Peace? I asked. Am I the keeper*
> *Of the heart's relics, blowing the dust*
> *In my own eyes?*
>
> From 'A Welsh Testament'

'R. S. Thomas ... poet priest'

Thomas is not a Welshman in the sense that his parishioners are Welshmen – as he well knows. But when Englishmen stare at him, and tow their caravans after them, and plant tax-evasion forests on the Welsh hills, and buy cottages in Welsh valleys for second homes, then Thomas is a Welshman through and through. The Welsh

Language Society and Meibion Glyndwr (Sons of Glyndwr) have agitated for years against this 'occupation'. Tony Heath wrote in *The Guardian* in 1988:

> The fuse was lit in December 1979 with the start of an arson campaign against second homes. More than 130 fires later, and with the arsonists still at large, the Rev. R. S. Thomas, Wales's leading poet, has supplied the detonator with a ringing declaration of support for the terrorists who, he claims, are the only true defenders of the Welsh language and culture. ... In a somewhat un-Christian aside the Rev. Thomas, who declines to be interviewed in English, called on local people to ostracise those moving into his area who lack bilingual ability.
>
> *The Guardian*, 12 May 1988

A Welsh journalist, Jan Morris, in the *Independent* took a more sympathetic view:

> The poet R. S. Thomas created a furore recently by expressing admiration for the arsonists who have been burning down English-owned holiday cottages (...) but more Welsh people agreed with him than Mrs Thatcher might find it comfortable to suppose.
>
> *The Independent*

 You could look for signs of this 'extremism' in R. S. Thomas's seemingly harmless country-parson poems. To what extent (if at all) are his early poems 'political'?

You might instead look at Seamus Heaney's later work and his 1975 collection *North*: have the 'troubles' in Northern Ireland made a political poet of this Ulsterman, who now lives in the Republic? Or at Scotsmen: Edward Lucie-Smith devotes Section 9 of his *British Poetry Since 1945* (Penguin) to Scotland. Is any Irish or Scottish poet as passionate as the Welshman, R. S. Thomas?

---

2 Poetry in time

An anthology of poetry generally has a unifying theme. There have been anthologies of love poems, war poems, poems of protest and pastoral poems. There are poems of this century, and of that reign, and of the other country. We have chopped up the 1900s into decades and talk about the poetry of the twenties and the fifties as if poets think in such terms.

The poetry of the 1930s is an especially happy hunting ground. There we can watch the world, with the dramatic irony of hindsight, sliding ineluctably to war. Auden called the 1930s in 'September 1, 1939': 'a low dishonest decade'.

If, to be significant, a poem must confront the significant issues of its time – social, political, life-and-death issues – then the 1930s gave rise to many a significant poem. Even Betjeman could not resist political commitment of sorts:

> *Come, friendly bombs, and fall on Slough*
> *It isn't fit for humans now,*
> *There isn't grass to graze a cow*
> *Swarm over, Death!*
>
> From 'Slough'

Robin Skelton, in his introduction to *Poetry of the Thirties* (Penguin), wrote:

> ... it sometimes seems as if the whole of the thirties generation was engaged in analysing its predicament and writing poetry and criticism about it, and was left-wing to a man ...
>
> *Poetry of the Thirties*, Penguin

Election results (as Skelton went on to say) prove that by no means everyone was a socialist, and many of Skelton's poets were Conservative voters. But, if the Spanish Civil War was a political litmus test, few turned so blue as to rally to Franco's Falangist cause. Few actually bore arms, but if words won wars the Republicans would have been the victors.

Skelton's anthology brings together 184 poems by 46 poets. He decided to include anything first printed in a book or periodical between 1 January 1930 and 31 December 1939 by poets born between 1904 and 1916. These, he judged, were men (sic) 'pitch-forked into a period of intense social tension in which to do their growing up'. This editorial policy unites the mighty with the slight.

Dylan Thomas broods rhetorically in 1935:

> *I have longed to move away*
> *From the hissing of the spent lie*
> *And the old terror's continual cry*
> *Growing more terrible as the day*
> *Goes over the hill into the deep sea;*

> *I have longed to move away*
> *From the reputation of salutes,*
> *For there are ghosts in the air*
> *And ghostly echoes on paper,*
> *And the thunder of calls and notes.*
>
> From 'I have longed to move away'

There are ghostly echoes of Eliot in Louis MacNeice's mid-1930s unseasonal Christmas thoughts:

> *The tin toys of the hawker move on the pavement inch by inch*
> *Not knowing that they are wound up; it is better to be so*
> *Than to be, like us, wound up and while running down to know.*
> *But everywhere the pretence of individuality recurs –*
> *Old faces frosted with powder and choked in furs*
> *The jutlipped farmer gazing over the humpbacked wall*
> *The commercial traveller joking in the urinal*
> *I think things draw to an end, the soil is stale –*
>
> From 'An Eclogue for Christmas'

By the end of the decade (if what follows is a guide) the time for poetry had passed. It was time to nail one's colours to the mast. Francis Scarfe cried 'Beauty, Boloney' and marched into war behind the avant-garde:

> *We prefer Modigliani*
> *Klee and Braque and Picasso*
> *to the Brutish Academy*
> *(may Lewis deal its knock-out blow)*
>
> *Lorca, Auden, Eluard*
> *Cummings, MacNeice, Apollinaire*
> *and Eliot are the giant hearts*
> *Slick, unvarnished debonair*
>
> *Meanwhile you can stuff the rest*
> *in the British Museum*
> *with fleas and laurels on their chest*
> *polybourgeoism philodumb*
>
> From 'Beauty, Boloney'

Whatever happened to Francis Scarfe? (or Bernard Gutteridge? or Robert Hamer? or Randall Swingler?) There are many poets among the 46 who owe their inclusion as much to their birthday as to their 'significance'. And even the big four (MacNeice, Spender, Auden and Day Lewis – referred to generically as 'Macspaunday' by the lonely Falangist, Roy Campbell) could commit atrocities in their passion. MacNeice's 'Bagpipe Music', Auden's 'A Communist to Others' and Day Lewis's 'The Magnetic Mountain: 20' are just three good reasons for more extensive scissorwork than Robin Skelton's.

 You might like the three above-mentioned poems. You might like many more of the poems of Gutteridge, Hamer, Swingler and company than of the 'big four'. There will certainly be poems you like, and perhaps many more that you dislike.

You could either make a choice of a small number of poems that you think capture the spirit of the 'low dishonest decade' especially well; or you could confine your attention to poems that presage war, or that relate to Spain, or that have to do with leadership. Whatever your theme, you will need to supply a rationale for your choice.

---

3 Poetry in place

When poets confront their times, like Old Testament prophets – particularly when they are persecuted or imprisoned for their pains – they stand a good chance of surviving those times. They take contemporary issues for their subject matter, and they write with a pen that has a cutting edge. They go to war, or to prison, or to broadcasting studios, and people listen.

Poets who stay at home, as a rule, make rather less impact. When the war, or the prison, or the broadcasters come to one's home (as they do in Ulster, and to a lesser extent, Wales), the poet may be heard by those who listen to poets. But, in the main, poets who write about a particular place – like Norman Nicholson of Cumbria, Glyn Hughes of the West Yorkshire Pennines, Iain Crichton-Smith of the Western Isles, even Charles Causley of Cornwall – are thought of as provincial poets. It is somehow harder to transcend place than time.

Foreign poets, whose home is 'abroad', have even more difficulty making themselves heard – though it helps if they write in English. Derek Walcott was born in St Lucia in the West Indies. He has lived and worked in Jamaica and Trinidad.

These countries are all members of the Commonwealth but it has taken time for Walcott's poetry to settle in Britain. His work was reviewed in Volume 21 of the *London Magazine*:

> JOHN FIGUEROA
>
> ## Dialect as Narrative
>
> Derek Walcott's work, considering he has published six volumes of poetry and two books of plays here, has curiously had less impact in England than in the United States. Yet he is a poet of outstanding gifts, in the English rather than the American style, whose deep feeling for his mixed St Lucian and Caribbean heritage is related to his concern for, and insight into, the general economic condition. Few contemporary writers combine such brilliance of natural imagery with so defined a sense of situation.
>
> *London Magazine*, Vol. 21, 1981

Walcott's poems can scarcely have been written anywhere else than in the Caribbean, not because they are written in dialect – they are not – but because the changes in the weather, the canvas sails, the teetering wooden shacks, the 'gossiping mosquitoes', the conch shells and the fishermen are all Caribbean, and because (just as Betjeman does, in Surrey and Berkshire), Walcott peppers his poems with place-names:

> *I looked from old verandas at*
> *verandas, sails, the eternal summer sea*
> *like a book left open by an absent master.*
> *And what if it's all gone,*
> *the hill's cut away for more tarmac,*
> *the groves all sawn,*
> *and bungalows proliferate on the scarred, hacked hillside,*
> *the magical lagoon drained*
> *for the Higher Purchase plan,*

> *and they've bulldozed and bowdlerized our Vigie,*
> *our* ocelle insularum, *our Sirmio,*
> *for a pink and pastel New Town where the shacks and huts stood.*
>
> From Chapter 23 of *Another Life*

There is more to Walcott, though, than a righteous, rightful rage against bulldozers and hoteliers and yachtsmen whose anchors kill the coral: in all his poems, there is sardonic comment on the ugly beauty, and the destructive creativity of all living things – comment that gives his poems universality. One does not have to have been cast away on a Caribbean beach or been confined indoors by tropical rain to make something of lines like these:

> *In the sun, the dog's faeces*
> *Crusts, whitens like coral.*
> *We end in earth, from earth began.*
> *In our own entrails, genesis.*
>
> From 'The Castaway'

> *So much rain, so much life like the swollen sky*
> *of this black August. My sister, the sun,*
> *broods in her yellow room and won't come out.*
> *Everything goes to hell; the mountains fume*
> *like a kettle, rivers overrun; still,*
> *she will not rise and turn off the rain.*
>
> From 'Dark August'

Caribbean, African, Indian writers have left home and settled in Britain to be nearer to their publishers and readers. V. S. Naipaul, the Trinidadian novelist, has achieved international status by leaving home – not so Derek Walcott. John Figueroa concluded his review article with these words:

> Walcott has told us that he has decided to stay at home and to work within his own domain; and he has kept the promise so to work as to touch all those who have the ears to hear his subtle music, and the eyes to see his bright, unselfindulgent images. In being so true to the sea grape and the star apple he should move many who know much better the pine and the oak.
>
> London Magazine, Vol. 21, 1981

Assuming *you* know the pine and the oak better than you know the sea grape and the star-apple, you will read the poems of Derek Walcott as an outsider, not as a 'belonger'. Wayne Brown assembled 50 of these poems (or extracts) for his *Selected Poetry* in the Heinemann Caribbean Writers Series. You might choose a small number of these that seem to you best to define the Caribbean experience. How do they do it, and what *is* that experience?

You could approach the poems of Dennis Brutus, in the African Writers Series, in the same way.

4 Thoughts on a second reading

Journalists, correspondents, advertisers, pamphleteers, storytellers, teachers and politicians: on the whole, these people strive for clarity. Some novelists express themselves in language that – though it is prose – is raised above the prosaic. Playwrights are committed to the spoken language, but, again, some playwrights make us work hard for meanings (as Stoppard does in *Jumpers* and *Hapgood*), or they write in prose concentrated to the point of poetry – as Beckett invariably does.

Still, when we read or hear prose, we expect to understand it the first time round. We do not expect to have to read a newspaper article a second time in order to understand it. Life is too short – and most news too trivial – for that. Nor do we expect to have to keep stopping to untangle knots in a novel – most novels are too long and few are 'significant' enough for that. And, though we can re-read a script, we cannot rewind a scene in a stage-play, as we can a video. It *must* work its effects on a first hearing, or be damned.

Most poems are short. Their lay-out on the page may attract or be off-putting, but they do not *have* to be plumbed on the first reading. Indeed, a poem that is drained of all its meaning the first time round is probably a rather insubstantial piece of work. It has to give enough of itself away, on a first reading, to tempt the reader to a second. A poem that is wilfully 'difficult' will not do this; it will deserve its own obscurity. The pity is that navel-gazing, essentially private poems give poetry a bad name. Students (and others) think all poems are difficult, and read horoscopes instead.

Philip Larkin has been almost as 'popular' a poet as John Betjeman because he was never wilfully obscure. He had something to say, and he said it lucidly and economically. A poem like 'Days', for example, is as simple as it looks. It yields up almost all of its 'idea' (and the poem is simple, in part, because there is just the one idea) at one go. Yet the idea teases, is whimsical, provoking – deep.

Philip Larkin, *The Independent*,
16 June 1988

Days

What are days for?
Days are where we live.
They come, they wake us
Time and time over.
They are to be happy in:
Where can we live but days?

Ah, solving that question
Brings the priest and the doctor
In their long coats
Running over the fields.

From *The Whitsun Weddings*, Faber, 1964

There is an ironical humour in the poem, as there is in almost all Larkin poems. That may be enough in itself to tempt us to read it again (that, and the fact that it is only ten lines long). All the words in the poem are common-or-garden words. Larkin never did indulge an ornate diction; nor did he run to images of an exotic sort – the poet was no more inclined to travel far from home than Derek Walcott. (Asked once whether he would not like to visit China, he said yes, so long as he could get there and back in a day.)

It is not because so many of Larkin's poems are intimations of mortality that they have what it takes to be lasting. They are about life and death – though not solemnly so. It is their very ordinariness, the fact that they express everyman's anxieties, that they ask shared questions, that they are so unassuming – and yet so probing – that will ensure that they are read a second, third and subsequent times. Larkin did not presume to knowledge that none of us has.

Ignorance

Strange to know nothing, never to be sure
Of what is true or right or real,
But forced to qualify or so I feel,
Or Well, it does seem so:
Someone must know.

Strange to be ignorant of the way things work:
Their skill at finding what they need,
Their sense of shape, and punctual spread of seed,
And willingness to change;
Yes, it is strange,

> *Even to wear such knowledge – for our flesh*
> *Surrounds us with its own decisions –*
> *And yet spend all our life on imprecisions,*
> *That when we start to die*
> *Have no idea why.*

From *The Whitsun Weddings,* Faber, 1964

 What is it about a poem that, at first sight, makes it seem 'difficult'? How far is this difficulty resolved on a second or third reading?

You might write about a clutch of Larkin poems (from *Whitsun Weddings* or *High Windows*, perhaps) from this point of view. What is unclear at first? Does re-reading help? Or are there questions left unanswered? If so, do you find this irritating or intriguing? Do you respond to all Larkin's poems in the same way?

---

5 Poetry out loud

I have said that a worthwhile poem cannot yield up all its meanings on a first reading. It may, however, be worth jeopardising some of these meanings in order to hear a poem read out loud by its author. What is true of the play is (almost as) true of the poem: however often one may read the words on the page, there is more meaning to be got from listening and watching than there is from reading.

Dylan Thomas was one of the most famous performers of poetry because he was one of the most inspired. He always rose to the occasion offered him by the BBC to read his poems (and short stories) on the radio – and *Under Milk Wood*, as we observed, was written with this medium in mind. The poet Michael Horowitz has said:

> Thomas knew what a ham he could be, but his recordings of 'Fern Hill', 'Do not go Gentle' and other of his finest poems have helped me enjoy and understand them on levels I'd never have plumbed otherwise.

The Independent, 10 June 1988

It was perhaps in a depressed or cynical moment that Thomas himself said that reading poems out loud was a largely worthless exercise consisting of 'travelling 200 miles just to recite, in my fruity voice, poems that would not be appreciated and could, anyway, be read in books'. It is true, Dylan Thomas was no more a native-born Welsh-speaker than his namesake R. S. Thomas was, but no Englishman could have done as much justice to the *sound* of the poems that was in the mind's ear of the poet at the time of writing as Dylan Thomas himself. Poetry is as near as language gets to music – especially lyrical and ballad poetry – and few would deny that a song is better sung, and a melody better played, than 'read in books'.

Dylan Thomas in performance, *The Independent,* 10 June 1988

Kevin Jackson asked a number of poets and performers whether they agreed with Dylan Thomas's 'mordant remarks'. Michael Horowitz referred to those poems that can *only* be appreciated in performance: dialect poems, West Indian 'dub' and Calypso-verse from Guyana. Edwin Morgan spoke of the function of poetry as 'entertainment', and Amelia Rosselli valued the way in which 'readings put you in closer touch with your audience and help keep you from being an ivory tower poet'. Douglas Dunn, friend of Philip Larkin and fellow Faber poet, was not so sure: on balance he was suspicious of poetry in performance:

DOUGLAS DUNN: *Born Renfrewshire 1942, now lives in Fife. Recent work includes Selected Poems 1964–83 (Faber)*

'My first candid reaction concerns money: you get paid for readings and it would be dishonest to forget that. On a more elevated level, critics are often fond of advocating that poetry should happen between the tongue and the teeth, rather than be some more kind of cerebral activity, and I think it can be a very healthy thing for a writer to be reminded in public about the sort of noises his poetry is making. TS Eliot talks about the auditory imagination, about the ways in which poetry can communicate before it is fully understood, and very often there is a great deal to be gained from hearing poems even in foreign languages that you

> don't understand, where what comes across is not exactly meaning but something more like gesture.
>
> I have a number of reservations, though. Readings can tempt a lot of poets into becoming out and out performers, writing just for immediate effect and so having to simplify their work; in effect, they end up writing the kind of poems which sound well read aloud. This obviously has dangers of ingratiation, or the boring sense of preaching to the converted. Also it can make a writer feel too much like The Poet, capital letters. Robert Frost once said that the word 'poet' is a praise word, it's not a word you'd use of yourself, and sometimes you see these very self-confident, thespian writers doing their all to be The Poet. One also tends to forget that some very good poets never gave readings: Larkin, for example, hardly ever gave public readings.'
>
> *The Independent,* 10 June 1988

Larkin is one of 25 poets represented in George MacBeth's poetry anthology *Poetry 1900 to 1975* (Longman with Faber & Faber) – and Dylan Thomas is another. The collection includes more than 200 poems, from those of Thomas Hardy to those of Seamus Heaney, and with one or two notable exceptions (C. Day Lewis, for example, and Siegfried Sassoon and Stephen Spender) it takes in all the major British poets of this century.

You could select poems from MacBeth's (or many another) anthology that, in your view, would lend themselves particularly well (or particularly ill) to performance. Are there poems, for example, that 'communicate' before they are 'fully understood'?

Explain fully the reasons for your selection of poems.

6 Abridgement

Editors, like MacBeth and yourself, have to have reasons for selecting one poem rather than another from what may be a large output. Larkin was very particular about including any poem in his collections with which he was not thoroughly satisfied. This meant that when Anthony Thwaite came to edit a collection of his poems, there were several that had not been published before. Thwaite had to decide whether inclusion of many juvenile, and some ill-tempered 'squibs', would enhance or damage Larkin's reputation. In the event, many of these were not included.

In the main, an editor selects or rejects whole poems. This is partly because few poets nowadays write very long poems, and partly because few editors feel comfortable with scissors. Only a poet as self-confident as Ezra Pound would have had the nerve to cut away two-thirds of *The Wasteland*, and reduce it to its present length. (Posterity probably has much to thank Pound for, in this respect, as Eliot had.) Not content with this reduction, however, MacBeth (in *Poetry 1900 to 1975*) butchers it still further, and in so doing, excises some of the very best lines.

In mitigation, MacBeth gives us 27 lines, out of something like 2,250, of John Betjeman's autobiographical poem *Summoned by Bells* (John Murray, 1960). And those lines do stand on their own, a discrete piece of blank verse, and they are worth having.

Another, much older, verse autobiography is William Wordsworth's *The Prelude (or Growth of a Poet's Mind)*. This runs to 14 'books', and takes in Wordsworth's childhood, his school-days, his years at Cambridge and his residence in London and in France; but it is Books 1 and 2 that are most often anthologised and set for study. Even these (taking us up to the poet's 'seventeenth year') are 1,117 blank-verse lines long.

Book 1 opens in characteristically Romantic vein with a flight from 'the vast city' – he should see it now! – to liberty and leisure in 'a green shady place'. Here the poet becomes convinced of a call to write poetry, but a fit subject eludes him. He aspires to write a philosophical poem but considers himself unequal to the task. At length, the poet realises that he must write about what he knows best: himself. It is what all writers are bound to do.

It is the River Derwent as it flows past Cockermouth that concentrates the poet's mind:

> *Oh, many a time have I, a five year's child,*
> *In a small mill-race severed from his stream,*
> *Made one long bathing of a summer's day;*
> *Basked in the sun, and plunged and basked again*
> *Alternate, all a summer's day, or scoured*
> *The sandy fields, leaping through flowery groves*
> *Of yellow ragwort; or when rock and hill,*
> *The woods, and distant Skiddaw's lofty height,*
> *Were bronzed with deepest radiance, stood alone*
> *Beneath the sky, as if I had been born*
> *On Indian plains, and from my mother's hut*
> *Had run abroad in wantonness, to sport,*
> *A naked savage, in the thunder shower.*
>
> Book 1, lines 288–300

Our noble savage goes to school in Hawkshead (1778–87), but there he learns (or will admit to learning) nothing that can be compared to what he learns from the Cumbrian hills and 'mountain brooks'. His childhood is an idyll of skating on frozen streams in the winter and of boating on Windermere in the summer. If any serious thought interrupts the round of pleasure-seeking, it is a reminder of the poet's duty to render an account of his stewardship of all the beauty and delight that have been entrusted to him.

There is much soul-searching, much nourishing of the poetic vision, so that 'the days flew by, and years passed on', and it was time to leave Cumbria for Cambridge:

> *It was a dreary morning when the wheels*
> *Rolled over a wide plain o'erhung with clouds,*
> *And nothing cheered our way till first we saw*
> *The long-roofed chapel of King's College lift*
> *Turrets and pinnacles in answering files,*
> *Extended high above a dusky grove.*
> *(...)*
> *As near and nearer to the spot we drew,*
> *It seemed to suck us with an eddy's force.*
> *Onward we drove beneath the Castle; caught*
> *While crossing Magdalene Bridge, a glimpse of Cam;*
> *And at the* Hoop *alighted, famous Inn.*
>
> Book 3, lines 1–6; 13–17

 It is something of a relief to read some story-telling narrative. Today's reader has a limited appetite for hymns to Nature. You could edit *The Prelude* to emphasise event and minimise musing: to reduce the whole to the size of the longer poems in MacBeth's anthology.

Alternatively, you could supply a prose paraphrase of the part of *The Prelude* that you find most pleasing – you need not confine yourself to Books 1 and 2.

You should explain your editorial procedure, or the basis of your choice of excerpt for paraphrase. (You might also address the question whether, by rendering blank verse as prose, any of the poetry is lost. What precisely does a paraphrase do to the original?)

---

7 Art and life

There was another William writing in Wordsworth's time, whose autobiography (in verse or not) it would have been good to have. We may learn much about William

Blake's point of view from his *Songs of Innocence and Experience*. We may infer his Wordsworth-like love of nature, his unsentimental respect for the simple and the childlike, and his essential devoutness combined with a suspiciousness of organised religion. There are critics and teachers (past and present) who would say that, as students of English, we should concern ourselves only with what we learn from the poems themselves: 'the text and nothing but the text'. Thus, we would read these lines from 'Holy Thursday' (*Songs of Innocence*):

> 'Twas on a Holy Thursday, their innocent faces clean
> The children walking two and two, in red and blue and green,
> Grey headed beadles walk'd before, with wands as white as snow,
> Till into the high dome of Paul's they like Thames' waters flow.
>
> O what a multitude they seem'd, these flowers of London town!
> Seated in companies they sit with radiance all their own.
> The hum of multitudes was there, but multitudes of lambs,
> Thousands of little boys and girls raising their innocent hands.
>
> William Blake, *Songs of Innocence*

and we *might* take note of the cruel irony in the reference to 'multitudes of lambs' (to the slaughter?), washed clean of the soot in which they sleep ('The Chimney Sweeper'). We *might* infer from 'The Echoing Green' that Blake thought children ought not to be marched in uniformed files, like the 'charter'd Thames' ('London'), behind old men with canes. And we *might* understand these canes to be symbols of blind oppression and the rigidity of the church's moral authority. We *might* even conclude that these were the same beadles who fed the innocents 'with cold and usurous hand' in 'Holy Thursday' (*Songs of Experience*).

But we would not learn from the poems themselves *why* Blake thought of childhood as he did, *why* his soul shrivelled in London, and *why* he scorned institutionalised religion.

We would read these lines from 'My Pretty Rose Tree' (*Songs of Experience*):

> A flower was offer'd to me,
> Such a flower as May never bore;
> But I said 'I've a Pretty Rose-tree,'
> And I passed the sweet flower o'er.
>
> Then I went to my Pretty Rose-tree,
> To tend her by day and by night;
> But my Rose turn'd away with jealousy,
> And her thorns were my only delight.
>
> William Blake, *Songs of Experience*

and we *might* conclude that Blake is giving sanction to marital fidelity: that in spite of all temptation, and subsequent rebuff, one ought to hold fast to one's marriage partner. We would not learn from this, or any other of his poems, that Blake was a passionate advocate of freedom in love as in all else. We could not infer from 'My Pretty Rose Tree' by itself that (in spite of his own lifelong fidelity to an illiterate market-gardener's daughter who bore him no children) Blake reproves himself for having been bound by the marriage ring. He had been made an offer he should *not* have refused, since innocent love, like innocent childhood play, ought *not* to be shut up in a pew.

Just as we needed to know why Joyce expressed himself so feelingly on the subject of 'entrapment' by Dublin, so we need to know why Blake was the radical critic of society and the symbolist that he was. Will we not understand his *Songs of Innocence and Experience* more penetratingly for knowing that:

> Blake received nothing resembling an ordinary education; and, being brought up in a Swedenborgian family, inclined to the cloudier parts of religion . . . his own reading, apart from the poets, included imaginative treatises on Gnosticism and Druidism . . . He fell under the influence of Gothic art, which became to him the supreme expression of truth . . .
>
> Blake began to meet persons, including Thomas Paine, favourable to the French Revolution . . .
>
> Blake's belief in physical freedom was part of his doctrine of enlightened liberty. One recalls with interest that during these years he knew Mary Wollstonecraft.
>
> George Sampson, *Concise Cambridge History of English Literature*, 3rd edn.

There are references here (to Swedenborgianism, to Gnosticism, to Mary Wollstonecraft) that one might have to look up elsewhere. But almost all one would need to know about Blake's life could be found in any reasonably comprehensive history of literature or biographical dictionary.

 Read a brief life history of William Blake, and identify the main 'influences' on his thinking. Choose a representative sample of his *Songs of Innocence and Experience* (to be found, for example, in *William Blake: Selected Poems*, ed. P. H. Butter, Dent, Everyman Classics), and trace the workings of these influences on the chosen poems.

Alternatively, you could seek out in his life the reasons for the change of mood between the engraving of *The Songs of Innocence* in 1789, and the addition of *The Songs of Experience* five years later. How does the change manifest itself in the poems?

---

8 An obituary

William Blake was influenced by Bunyan, Isaac Watts and the Bible. Blake and the Bible were among the influences on a young poet and artist of Russian Jewish ancestry, Isaac Rosenberg (1890–1918). Blake the artist was almost as big an influence on the young Rosenberg as Blake the amateur mythologist. Both men lived in London, and both moved in backwaters of the literary mainstream. But not only one hundred years separated the two men: Isaac Rosenberg lived to fight in the trenches of the First World War – and to die in them.

Of the poets who died in that war – Rosenberg, Wilfred Owen, Rupert Brooke, Edward Thomas – Owen is undoubtedly the best known. Indeed, his poems are more prominent in anthologies of twentieth-century poetry than those of the poets who fought and survived – Siegfried Sassoon, Robert Graves, Edmund Blunden and Herbert Read.

Rupert Brooke was established as a poet before war broke out. He had been idolised for his debonair good looks and public school and varsity polish. Edward Marsh had included him among his Georgian poets; indeed, it was Brooke who set the tone of the collections. When war was declared, Brooke wrote sonnets only one degree less jingoistic than the songs of Henry ('Play up, play up, and play the Game!') Newbolt.

> *Now, God be thanked who has matched us with His hour,*
> *And caught our youth, and wakened us from sleeping*
>
> From 'Peace'

> *Blow out, you bugles, over the rich Dead!*
> *There's none of these so lonely and poor of old,*
> *But, dying, has made us rarer gifts than gold.*
>
> From 'The Dead'

> *If I should die, think only this of me:*
> *That there's some corner of a foreign field*
> *That is for ever England.*
>
> From 'The Soldier'

It was poetry of the sort that Owen was to write that made Brooke's refined verses seem strained, artificial and 'pre-war'. (It has taken time for us to see that the eclipse ought not to have been total.)

Wilfred Owen

Owen had written some publishable poems before he joined up. These included the sonnet '1914', which might have been written by Brooke or another of the Georgians:

> *War broke: and now the Winter of the world*
> *With perishing great darkness closes in.*
> *The foul tornado, centred at Berlin,*
> *Is over all the width of Europe whirled,*
> *Rending the sails of progress.*
>
> From '1914'

Owen was steeped in Romantic poetry, and in that of Keats in particular. He had been determined for some time that he would be a poet. He had written to his cousin from Bordeaux, in July 1915:

> I don't imagine that the German War will be affected by my joining in, but I know my own future Peace will be. I wonder that you don't ply me with this argument: that Keats remained absolutely indifferent to Waterloo and all that commotion.

The argument would have been to no avail. He had passed a year in 'fine-contemptuous nonchalance'; now it was time to seek out the excitement that he admitted (in a letter to his sister) was necessary to his happiness.

If he went to war in much the same spirit as Brooke, his experience of the trenches set him swiftly on a new course. But it was Sassoon – an older man, and an already published poet – who showed him the way. Owen met Sassoon at a war hospital, near Edinburgh. It was here that Owen wrote what is perhaps the single best-known poem to come out of the First World War: 'Anthem for Doomed Youth'.

'Dulce et Decorum Est', 'Inspection', 'Futility', 'Strange Meeting' and others all followed in rapid succession. Patriotism gave way to anger, and pity; the sonnet gave way to reportage. The one thing needful was to take the invalid Sassoon's place as the unofficial laureate of the horror. That he died within a week of the armistice only confirmed his place with Keats among the poets-as-tragic-heroes.

Rosenberg has been less noticed, though the critic G. S. Fraser judged him to have had 'even more than Owen, the makings of a major figure'. It may be that his poems are less immediate – less accessible – than Owen's. That he was a private – not an officer like Owen, like Sassoon and like Graves – may be another reason for neglect. 'Break of Day in the Trenches' is one of his better-known pieces.

> *The darkness crumbles away –*
> *It is the same old druid Time as ever.*
> *Only a live thing leaps my hand –*
> *A queer sardonic rat –*
> *As I pull the parapet's poppy*
> *To stick behind my ear.*
> *Droll rat, they would shoot you if they knew*
> *Your cosmopolitan sympathies (...)*
>
> From 'Break of Day in the Trenches'

 Choose one of the poets who died in the First World War represented in the anthologies (*Up the Line to Death*, for example, edited by Brian Gardner). On the basis of a small sample of his poems – and perhaps a few biographical data – write an obituary of the poet, an appreciation or critic's tribute. Make the poems themselves the primary evidence for your estimate of the man.

FOUR

Non-fiction

What is non-fiction?

This may sound like a question that answers itself. If there is one thing that non-fiction must not be, it is *fiction*. In practice, as we have seen, much fiction (particularly much modern fiction) purports to be history, or the fruit of personal experience. For every *Nice Work* by David Lodge there is a *Lost Father* by Marina Warner.

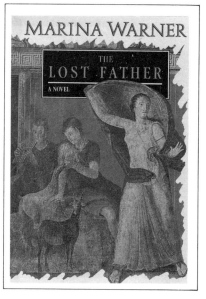

Nice Work David Lodge: *Secker*
Confrontation between a deconstructionalist, feminist lecturer, Robyn Penrose, and a realist, capitalist factory director whom she is forced to shadow as part of an Industry Year PR exercise. Successfully relates their thinking and politics to a post-industrial and money-mad Britain.
It's a love story, too.

The Lost Father
Marina Warner: *Chatto*
To escape the menace of Fascism Davide Pittagora left Italy for America but found nothing but hardship and humiliation. With his family, he returned to his homeland and met his death in a duel. His granddaughter finds the story mystifying and reconstructs her own version of the family history. A kaleidoscope of unforgettable characters.

Advertisements in *The Times Educational Supplement*, 21 October 1988

The Lost Father is a work of fiction – it is a novel. There is no doubt about this. But Warner's novel grew out of interest in, and research into, the life and times of her grandparents. Another recent novel, Anthony Sher's *Middlepost*, sprang from just the same interest. No one would accuse his actor's journal, *Year of the King*, of being fiction (see page 108), but the seeds of *Middlepost* are sown in that book.

Another of the novels short-listed for the 1988 Booker Prize (with the Lodge and Warner) was *The Satanic Verses* by Salman Rushdie.

> Two Bombay citizens, one 'a brown Uncle Tom', the other an Indian film star, fall from a sabotaged plane, and land miraculously on the beach at Hastings. They are reincarnated as the angel Gibreel and the devil Saladin.

There is no question that this is a work of fiction. Rushdie's *Midnight's Children* won the Booker Prize in 1981. The newspaper *India Today* said of it:

> ... it is in fictional terms one of the most ferocious indictments of India's evolution since Independence.
>
> *India Today*

Midnight's Children was a work of fiction; but names are named, and Mrs Ghandhi is identifiable as the lady with the silver streak in her hair. The Indian authorities didn't like *Midnight's Children*. And the Pakistani authorities didn't like *Shame*, the novel 'about' Zia's Pakistan that followed in 1983. Malcolm Bradbury said of *Shame* in *The Guardian*:

> The theme is shame and shamelessness, born from the violence which is modern history ... Rushdie shows us with what fantasy our sort of history must now be written.
>
> *The Guardian*

Where does history stop and fantasy start? Much modern journalism is a subtle blend of history and fantasy. The authorities didn't like Rushdie's novels because they saw – though they were works of fiction (the author, his publishers and the Booker judges said so), plainly they were not *non-fiction* – that they were works of inspired journalism.

We trust that the news that we read in newspapers is not out-and-out fiction, but we are sophisticated enough to know that it is not simple *fact*. We know perfectly well that a piece of news that we hear on the radio first thing in the morning:

> The month's unemployment figures show a slight rise in the numbers out of work, but the long-term unemployment trend is down for the fourth month in succession. The Employment Secretary said the overall picture was 'very heartening'.

can look very different in the morning's newspapers:

> **'Heartening' drop in unemployment**
>
> There has been a marginal rise in the number of men and women out of work, owing to what a spokesman at the Department of Employment called 'seasonal factors'. But the numbers of those who have been out of work for twelve months or more continue to drop, as the Employment Secretary forecast they would. 'The government's strategy is on course,'

> **JOBLESS UP YET AGAIN!**
>
> The numbers of men and women out of work are up by 23,000 over last month. No amount of fudge by this government can disguise the harsh reality of this appalling waste of

We tend to read the newspaper whose view of the world we share – and of course we do not only read newspapers for news that we can as easily catch by turning on the radio or television. Reporters gather 'facts' and retail them on the instant. The medium is a matter (more or less) of indifference.

Journalism is something else again. The journalist writes to a deadline – but it is measured in hours or days, not minutes. He or she may be a travel writer, a political commentator, an art critic or a biographer. And he or she may well write the kind of book (about travel, politics, art or 'personalities') that will line the non-fiction shelves in the bookshops and be set for study by students of English.

Park Honan is a Professor of English and American Literature and a writer of literary biography. In a recent article (in *Words International*), he describes how fact was made fiction (by the David Lodge of *Nice Work*):

> It is a strange, unnerving experience to find one's life the subject of fiction. I discovered this when my friend David Lodge turned my trauma in coming to teach at Birmingham into the comic trauma of Morris Zapp. Readers of CHANGING PLACES will recall the deluge of tobacco tins on Zapp's head, just after he enters his tutorial room at Rummidge. In fact, when I reached Birmingham University in 1968 the English Department secretary, who knew nothing of my appointment,

> sent me down a corridor to a door with the sign 'MR. GREEN' on it. Had I lost my own name? Feeling rattled I entered Mr. Green's room – into which he perhaps had flung a hand-grenade just as he left – and amidst many sad fragments of cardboard boxes, I opened an overhead cabinet. A tobacco tin fell out and hit me on the head. 'Then and only then,' I told David Lodge, 'I knew my flight from America was over: I knew I was in the English Midlands'. David turned all that into the shower on Zapp's head.
>
> <div align="right"><i>Words International</i>, Vol. 1, No. 3, p. 6</div>

We may sometimes suspect that the same process is at work in newspaper offices. After all, many novelists double as journalists, and many journalists are novelists *manqués*.

The biographer, though, must surely be true to the evidence. If you wrote an 'obituary' of one of the poets of the First World War (see page 86), your evidence will have been the poems themselves. Park Honan wrote a biography of the poet and essayist Matthew Arnold. To do this, he had (of course) to read Arnold's poems and essays –and much else that Arnold wrote and was written about him:

> I had newly released journals and diaries with material on Arnold's childhood, letters by Arnold and his friends and family, many reports about him, and new evidence concerning virtually every aspect of his life. But no child in history has ever matured in a cultural, emotional or intellectual vacuum; and I saw that if I darted back at the past in a casual, backward-looking manner, quoted letters or diaries here and there, and did little to give a sense of Arnold developing in a historical environment, I could not show how several forces influenced my subject almost simultaneously. I needed a biographical form that would be conducive to a finer clarity and accuracy; such a form would be based on enough research into Arnold's family, his environment, and contemporary society to help me suggest what is knowable about his own continuing 'historical present', the life that he lived, with an unpredictable future ahead. I could then show, as accurately as the evidence would let me, how persons, events, as well as his plans, ideas, and unsolved problems impinged upon him in history. The test of my own prose, I thought, should not be whether it was casual or chatty or smart or had 'flow', but whether it would be delicately accurate enough to do justice to my evidence.
>
> <div align="right"><i>Words International</i>, Vol. 1, No. 3, p. 8</div>

The question that Honan faced – that any biographer faces – was how far he was justified in attempting to write insightfully about Arnold's 'inner' life, and how far he should confine himself to 'externalities'. Bernard Crick, who wrote a biography of George Orwell (*George Orwell: A Life*, Penguin, 1982), adopted the latter course on the grounds that: 'Our human identity consists in relationships, not in inwardness.' Crick did not feel that it was any business of his to engage in 'guesswork'. His job was to 'stand outside Orwell, noting his behaviour'. Honan dismissed this limited vision of the biographer's role with two tart questions:

> Is all inwardness a fiction? Or is it just that, in an era of scientific positivism, Xeroxes, and footnotes, Mr Crick is impatient with what he finds hard to judge?

(p. 9)

The writer of autobiography does not face this problem – nor does the travel-writer who sets no great store by objectivity.

Cider with Rosie has proved to be one of the most popular works of autobiography ever to have celebrated childhood. It was first published in 1959, up to 40 years after the episodes and impressions it purports to record. In a disarming note at the beginning, Laurie Lee issues this warning:

> The book is a recollection of early boyhood and some of the facts may be distorted by time.

Would that all writers of autobiography (biography too, if it comes to that) were as honest as this. Whole conversations are (apparently) faithfully recalled, as if *Cider with Rosie* was a novel in the same way that *Middlepost* and *The Lost Father* are novels. H. E. Bates, novelist, called it a prose poem.

Its sequel, *As I Walked Out One Midsummer Morning* (André Deutsch, 1969) is the memoir of a traveller's love-affair with Spain. It is one step closer to 'straight' non-fiction than *Cider with Rosie*, but both books demonstrate that the line between what we call fiction and what we call non-fiction is as fine as that between what we call prose and what we call poetry.

What do we look for in non-fiction?

Clarendon's *History*, Addison's Essays for *The Spectator*, Boswell's *Life of Johnson*, de Quincey's *Confessions*, Hazlitt's *Table Talk*, Carlyle's *Heroes and Hero Worship*, Sassoon's *Memoirs*, Eliot's *Notes* and Orwell's social criticism have all been thought of as 'literature', or perhaps more precisely as *belles-lettres*. They must all have been studied at some time, though non-fiction written before about 1900 is read mostly by antiquarians now.

Examination boards have not always allowed for, or specified, non-fiction titles among those set for study. Now that they do, there is uncertainty as to which works of non-fiction qualify as 'literature'. Is such a work one written:

1 By a writer who also writes novels, plays or poems?

2 By a writer *about* a novelist, playwright or poet?

3 By an actor, musician or critic, or someone otherwise artistic or creative? Or

4 By an author whose work is adjudged by literary *cognoscenti* to be 'fine writing'?

Each of the texts considered later in this chapter falls into one or another of these categories, with the possible exception of the Maya Angelou. Perhaps for this, the first of three volumes of autobiography, we need a fifth category: for works of 'gutsy humanity' or something of the sort.

The reviews of non-fiction books transmit mixed messages (the following are from the *South East Arts Review*, Issues 17, 19 and 20 respectively):

Book Reviews

Portrait of a Kentish Village: Michael McNay
(*Gollancz – hdbk £8.95*)
Mr McNay's village is typical of a small community in what was once the Garden of England, but it is now the juggernaut corridor to the Continent. Not quite, typically, however, since East Malling, the subject of the book, lies just off the main road and has thus been spared the fate of nearby villages like Wateringbury which lie slap in the path of the traffic. Like a good portraitist, the author contemplates his sitter from all sides – first as a farming community which has seen hops and cherries come and now almost go at the whim of EEC regulations, then as a religious unit subject to today's centrifugal forces, and an administrative unit in which the parish councillor feels almost helpless in front of the tiers of authority ranged above him (...) Michael McNay writes in a highly readable way (...) His book is of relevance to small threatened communities everywhere, and should be required reading for the bureaucrats whose job it is to implement the structure plan for Kent (...)
Keith Spence

Ideas and the Novel: Mary McCarthy
(*Weidenfeld & Nicholson – hdbk £4.95*)
(...) This book is certainly a stimulating read, full of controversial arguments and seminal thought, and despite its rather biased view that nothing of value in fiction is being written any more (what is this generation coming to!) will prove invaluable to students of 19th century literature as the work of a brilliantly analytical mind, as well as an absorbing read for others with a taste for the postmortem.

Rhona Martin

A Language not to be Betrayed – Selected Prose of Edward Thomas: Edited by Edna Longley
(Carcanet – hdbk £9.95)

It was Thomas's poetry that finally established his reputation, for most of us forget that before this he was an acknowledged prose writer and in particular a respected book reviewer. Forced to write more than a million words of reviews in order to earn a living, it is not surprising that many of them now appear stunted. No doubt they served their purpose as a comment on the literary scene, but they are of little relevance when read for their critical acumen today. To see the critic at work one has to go to the longer books, such as his study of Swinburne. (...) Thomas is best remembered, as a prose writer, for his books on the countryside and there are generous selections in this anthology. They are still a pleasure to read because of Thomas's enthusiasm and skill; but it is hard to believe in this idealised, rustic landscape, that neglects the hard life and poverty of the farm labourer (...)
Roland John

South East Arts Review, Issues 17, 19 and 20

A *Guardian* journalist writing about a Kent village under siege, a novelist lambasting the modern novel, and a poet viewing and reviewing the pastoral and the literary scene – all three books *might* have qualified on the grounds of authorship or subject for set book status, as long as they were not *dis*qualified by their being: 'required reading for bureaucrats', 'rather biased', and 'of little relevance' – not to say 'idealised' – respectively. Certainly we do not disqualify Kafka's novels, Strachey's biographies and Edward Thomas's poems on these grounds.

Peter Abbs believes very firmly that English in schools has to do with 'literature'. English as a discipline is:

> That formal and informal process of responding to and reconstructing the inherited store of myths, legends, stories, novels, poems, plays, the collective store of narrative and metaphor.
>
> 'English as Art', in *Words*, No. 8, January 1986

On the face of it, this would seem to exclude non-fiction such as that reviewed above. But Abbs quotes the novelist E. M. Forster, on the novelist Virginia Woolf, to this effect:

> She liked receiving sensations – sights, sounds, tastes – passing them through her mind, where they encountered theories and memories, and then bringing them out again, through a pen, on a bit of paper. Now began the higher delights of authorship. For these pen-marks on paper were only the prelude to writing, little more than marks on a wall. They had to be combined, arranged, emphasized here, eliminated there, new relationships had to be generated, new pen-marks born, until out of the interactions, something, one thing, one, arose. This one thing, whether it was a novel or an essay or a short story or a biography or a private paper to be read to her friends, was, if it was successful, itself analogous to a sensation. Although it was so complex and intellectual, although it

might be large and heavy with facts, it was akin to the very simple things which had started it off, to the sights, sounds, tastes. It could be best described as we describe them. For it was not about something. It was something.

Words, No. 8, January 1986

The mode in which Virginia Woolf wrote was of so little moment to Forster that he did not even waste commas holding one mode apart from another. What mattered was not whether the work was fiction or 'heavy with facts', but that it had 'something' that had been experienced, or 'sensed', that could in turn be sensed by the reader. In Peter Abbs' words, a piece of writing is literature when it is 'resonant with meaning'.

We need not concern ourselves, then, with what a piece of non-fiction is 'about', nor with who wrote it. These things would concern us if we were sociologists or historians interested in 'facts'. As students of literature, we are interested in feelings. As long as the writers of non-fiction set out to do the same job as the writers of novels, plays and poems – in the same resonant language of feeling – we need be no more comma-conscious than Forster.

How might one write about non-fiction?

1 Travel writing

Laurie Lee left the village of Slad in Gloucestershire in 1934. He 'walked out one midsummer morning', a youth of 19, bound for Spain. He returned to Spain, 50 years later, before the filming of his book for BBC television. Heather Lawton interviewed Laurie Lee for the *Radio Times*, and quoted his impressions of the country thus:

> It's disturbing returning, particularly to the South. Tourism has imposed self-consciousness upon an innocent coast. It's one of the worst things that could have happened next to a nuclear war. It has destroyed people's pride. I remember in the '30s walking from Gibraltar to Malaga in five days along what is now the Costa del Sol. The coast was empty. I would pass through villages of starving fishermen. The only food to eat if you were lucky was sardines. I would just walk into the sea, put it over my head and breathe the salt-stung neutral nowhere, and there was no-one else, no-one but me on that coast.
>
> *Radio Times,* 3–9 January 1987

Rear cover of *As I Walked Out One Midsummer Morning*

One might agree with Laurie Lee that the appearance of the coastline has not been improved by the stacks of hotels, like filing-cabinets, that line the beach – though the fishermen's grandchildren probably prefer eating to starvation. But one would probably not share his dismay, on arrival at the Costa del Sol, at finding other people there. We do not all choose to travel alone. Few of those who earn a living in the package-holiday business (as I do not) will even agree with him (as I do) about the hotels.

Sardinia has changed rather less in 70 years than Spain had in 50. D. H. Lawrence and his wife visited Sardinia early in their long odyssey in Europe, Australia and America. Cagliari is a thriving port at the southern end of the island, and the sea-link with Sicily. In the early 1920s, it was 'rather bare, rather stark, rather cold and yellow – somehow like Malta, without Malta's foreign liveliness'. Lawrence, actually, rather liked Cagliari, for much the same reasons that Laurie Lee liked the coast-road to Malaga. It was (in Lee's words) 'innocent, unravaged, undefiled' – or, as we should say, 'unspoilt'. Lawrence writes about Cagliari thus, in Chapter 3 of *Sea and Sardinia*:

> *Strange, stony Cagliari. We climbed up a street like a cork-screw stairway. (. . .) Cagliari is very steep. Half-way up there is a strange place called the bastions, a large level space like a drill ground with trees, curiously suspended over the town (. . .) What is so curious is that this Terrace or bastion is so large, like some big recreation ground, that it is almost dreary, and one cannot understand its being suspended in mid-air. Down below is the little circle of the harbour. To the left, a low, malarial-looking sea plain, with tufts of palm-trees and Arab-looking houses (. . .)*
>
> *Curious the children in Cagliari. The poor seem thoroughly poor, bare-footed urchins, gay and wild in the narrow dark streets. But the more well-to-do children are so fine: so extraordinarily elegantly dressed. It quite strikes one of a heap. Not so much the grown-ups. The children. All the* chic, *all the fashion, all the originality is expended on the children. And with a great deal of success. Better than Kensington Gardens very often. And they promenade with Papa and Mama with such alert assurance, having quite brought it off, their fashionable get-up. Who would have expected it?*

Penguin edition, pp. 61, 64

Lawrence was an observant tourist (he would not have called himself a tourist, of course, of any sort). His eye caught, and his pen recorded, more than any modern view-finder could frame. If one reads *Sea and Sardinia* for views, however, it is less for Lawrence's record of sights and sounds – fascinating though these are – than for his sudden enthusiasms and queer antipathies. A travel writer (like Lawrence) reveals a lot about himself in his writing – as he must if his interest extends beyond the facts in a gazetteer.

> *We go down the steep streets, smelly, dark, dank, and very cold. No wheeled vehicle can scramble up them, presumably. People live in one room. Men are combing their hair or fastening their collars in doorways (. . .)*
>
> *The crowd is across the road, under the trees near the sea. On this side stroll occasional pedestrians. And I see my first peasant in costume. He is an elderly, upright, handsome man, beautiful in the black-and-white costume. He wears the full-sleeved white shirt and the close black bodice of thick, native frieze cut low (. . .) The drawers are banded below the knee into tight black frieze gaiters. On his head he has the long black stocking-cap, hanging down behind. How handsome he is, and so beautifully male!*
>
> *In the morning the sun was shining from a blue, blue sky, but the shadows were*

> *deadly cold, and the wind like a flat blade of ice. We went out running to the sun. The hotel could not give us coffee and milk: only a little black coffee. So we descended to the sea front again, to the Via Roma, and to our café. It was Friday: people seemed to be bustling in from the country with huge baskets.*
>
> *The Café Roma had coffee and milk, but no butter.*

(pp. 65, 68, 69)

Lawrence did not fasten on flattering detail, nor did he pay compliments where no compliment was due ('We look at the shops. But there is not much to see. Little frowsy provincial shops, on the whole'). He would not have succeeded as a package-tour company's copywriter; he was far too honest. Being Lawrence, too, he noticed people rather pointedly: their bearing and their wearing. ('When all is said and done, the most attractive costume for women, in my eye, is the tight little bodice and the many pleated skirt.')

You could make your own selection of extracts from *Sea and Sardinia*, and show what it is that Lawrence reveals about himself in them. (You could, of course, do the same of *As I Walked Out* . . . .)

Alternatively, you could write as a tour-operator, taking Lawrence (or Lee) as a point of departure, and re-casting their observations in more positive terms. What is there in Lawrence's (or Lee's) record that would lend itself to direct quotation so as to present Sardinia (or Spain) in the most favourable light? What aspect of the record would need to be suppressed or re-interpreted?

---

2 Author bias

Lawrence wrote with a decided bias, but his book is the richer for it. When a Sicilian carpenter irritates him, he damns him (and all his kind) behind his back:

> . . . one should never let these fellows get into conversation nowadays. They are no longer human beings. They hate one's Englishness, and leave out the individual.

Which is precisely what Lawrence does when one man multiplied becomes 'these fellows'. We mostly forgive him his bias (where we would not forgive prejudice), because his judgements are based on experience, not hearsay. His opinions are first-hand.

When an author writes a biography of someone he has known well (as James Boswell did of Samuel Johnson), and perhaps lived with and suffered, again we expect the account to be biased. It is impossible to be in the company of another person (parent, husband, wife, close friend) for many years and to be altogether unaffected. One would not be writing the biography in the first place if one had not been affected by its subject. Middleton Murry's memoir of his wife Katherine Mansfield is valuable for an understanding of Katherine the writer, but it can never be the 'definitive' biography because Murry was too close. Anyone who attempted to write *the* biography of Katherine Mansfield would need to refer to it, but allowance would need to be made for the very proper 'bias' of a proud, if not always comprehending, husband.

If literati doubt whether a work of biography qualifies as 'literature', historians (of the academic sort, at least) question whether it is history. When people who are historians write about things, we can expect them to write with objectivity; but when historians, who are people, write about other people, we should expect there to be a measure of author bias. The observed has an effect on the observer in historiography as in physics.

Lytton Strachey was (with E. M. Forster, the Woolfs, the Bells and John Maynard Keynes) a member of the loose-knit 'Bloomsbury Group'. Almost anything written by a member of this group (and their friends, and sons and daughters) is on-the-instant literature. Products of the late Victorian middle class, group members professed contempt for all things Victorian and middle class. Strachey was less a historian than a 'man of letters' who turned his hand to biography (or 'psychography' as he called it, donning the mantle of the psychoanalyst, after Freud). His *Eminent Victorians* was published in 1918. This was a systematic 'de-bagging' (the critic Angus Ross's word), or de-bunking (to misuse Henry Ford's), of three of the heroes and one heroine of Victorian mythology: Dr Thomas Arnold, the headmaster; Florence Nightingale; General Gordon ('of Khartoum'), and Henry Edward Manning, the Cardinal. The first paragraph of Strachey's portrait of Florence Nightingale is instructive:

> *Everyone knows the popular conception of Florence Nightingale. The saintly, self-sacrificing woman; the delicate maiden of high degree who threw aside the pleasures of a life of ease to succour the afflicted; the Lady with the Lamp, gliding through the horrors of the hospital at Scutari, and consecrating with the radiance of her goodness the dying soldier's couch – the vision is familiar to all. But the truth is different. The Miss Nightingale of fact was not as facile fancy painted her. She worked in another fashion, and towards another end; she moved under the stress of an impetus which finds no place in the popular imagination. A Demon possessed her. Now demons,*

whatever else they may be, are full of interest. And so it happens that in the real Miss Nightingale there was more that was interesting than in the legendary one; there was also less that was agreeable.

Strachey sought to unpick the 'popular conception' of each of his four subjects. Thus, Dr Arnold was thought 'pompous', Miss Nightingale was a 'busybody', General Gordon was an habitual drunkard, and Cardinal Manning was more ambitious than it was wholesome for a clergyman to be.

Biography is 'popular' history. If Strachey had been alive in 1979, he would almost certainly have written the scripts for the BBC television series about the hero of his own day, the 'Welsh Wizard' David Lloyd George, or he would have written the book (that David Benedictus based on the scripts of Elaine Morgan) that was published in paperback (in 1981) by Sphere Books.

> In this sensational biography David Benedictus gives a candid and compelling portrayal of the twentieth century's most fascinating and controversial political leader.

So sings the blurb. Can a 'sensational', 'candid and compelling portrayal' not be biased? Can it not be a portrait sat for in a certain pose, painted from a certain angle, and seen in a certain light?

You could judge for yourself what Lytton Strachey thought of Florence Nightingale (or any other of his eminent Victorians – or, indeed, of Queen Victoria herself, whose biography by Strachey was published in 1921). What is the nature of his 'bias', and what is its effect on our sympathies?

Or you might defend *Eminent Victorians* as literature, or mount a critical attack on it (or on 'Lloyd George') as history.

3 The selective memory

Lawrence wrote a lot about himself in his travelogue – but incidentally. Strachey revealed much about himself in his biographical sketches of Victorian 'legends' – but, again, such revelation is incidental.

We should be surprised if an autobiography was not biased. Self-revelation is central to autobiography, not incidental. How can one render an account of what one does, and thinks, and sees, and says, and not be partisan? We do not expect a writer to be able to stand outside himself, as Crick claims to stand outside Orwell. He must have a point of view, and he must express it. A persistently reserved judgement is rather more tiresome than praiseworthy.

Graham Greene was the Grand Old Man of English letters long before he was 80 in 1984. He had become an institution, and Greeneland, a seedy backwater somewhere between Panama and Vietnam, was clearly identifiable on the literary map.

Graham Greene, *The Times*, 16 October 1986

Greene had not finished writing worthwhile novels, even at the age of 80. Yet his autobiography, *A Sort of Life*, was published in 1971, when he was only 66. It starts, conventionally enough, with childhood's first memories in Berkhampsted when he wore a pinafore and his fair curls fell down about his neck. It does not come to an end at an age when most men retire, and he was a Companion of Honour with screen-plays and war-service and the Hawthornden Prize behind him. He brings the narrative to an end in the trough of 'failure' following the publication of his first, unresounding novel, *The Man Within*, in 1929 when he was a newly-married man of 25. The record follows him through school and university and on to the staff of *The Times*. An autobiography may contain fewer errors of fact than a biography, and, as Greene says, it may be more selective and end prematurely, but if *A Sort of Life* is the autobiography of a novelist, it ends almost before it has begun.

Penguin Books call it 'autobiography', whilst Greene himself calls it an 'essay'. Whatever it is, we would not be without it, because it contains the essential Graham Greene: a well connected young man, dogged by depression. Perhaps the most celebrated episode in the book concerns his experiment in suicide:

> *I put the muzzle of the revolver into my right ear and pulled the trigger. There was a minute click, and looking down at the chamber I could see that the charge had moved into the firing position. I was out by one. I remember an extraordinary sense of jubilation, as if carnival lights had been switched on in a dark drab street. My heart knocked in its cage, and life contained an infinite number of possibilities. It was like a young man's first successful experience of sex – as if among the Ashridge beeches I had passed the test of manhood. I went home and put the revolver back in the corner-cupboard.*
>
> *This experience I repeated a number of times. At fairly long intervals I found myself craving for the adrenalin drug, and I took the revolver with me when I returned to Oxford. There I would walk out from Headington towards Elsfield down what is now a wide arterial road, smooth and shiny like the walls of a public lavatory. Then it was a sodden unfrequented country lane. The revolver would be whipped behind my back, the chamber twisted, the muzzle quickly and surreptitiously inserted in my ear beneath the black winter trees, the trigger pulled.*
>
> *Slowly the effect of the drug wore off – I lost the sense of jubilation, I began to receive from the experience only the crude kick of excitement. It was the difference between love and lust.*
>
> Penguin edition, p. 94

Such an exceptional young man was bound to grow up to be an exceptional old man. As an elderly man of 66, he was determined to write an exceptional sort of autobiography:

> There is a fashion today among many of my contemporaries to treat the events of their past with irony. It is a legitimate method of self-defence. 'Look how absurd I was when I was young' forestalls cruel criticism but it falsifies history. We were not Eminent Georgians. Those emotions were real when we felt them. Why should we be more ashamed of them than of the indifference of old age? I have tried, however unsuccessfully, to live again the follies and sentimentalities and exaggerations of the distant time, and to feel them, as I felt them then, without irony.
>
> Penguin edition, rear cover

What emotions *did* Greene feel that were so 'real'? What follies are revealed in his account? What sentimentalities, and what exaggerations? Is it possible to tell? Does he succeed in feeling them all over again 'without irony'?

The above is a straightforward assessment of the author's success in fulfilling his 'intention'. More creatively, you could rewrite a passage of *A Sort of Life* in the ironical manner in which one of his 'contemporaries' might have written it.

4 Interview with the author

Graham Greene always was a secretive sort. Paul Hogarth painted certain of the settings of Greene's novels, and the paintings were exhibited in London. Bryan Appleyard wrote in *The Times* before the exhibition: 'The opening will be attended by the great man himself who is making one of his rare visits to London.' Greene wrote letters to *The Times* from his home in Antibes, but he was reluctant to give interviews. Greene wrote a foreword and commentary on Hogarth's paintings, and the collection was published as a book entitled *Graham Greene Country* by Pavilion in 1986. Appleyard wrote:

> ... on his latest visit to London he has reverted to something like his old secretive style. He had observed that every time he brought out a book there was a huge demand for interviews in expectation that it would be his last. This time a message came from his sister that he did not wish to talk.
>
> *The Times*, 16 October 1986

J. D. Salinger, author of *The Catcher in The Rye*, is even more reclusive. One might as well attempt to interview a Trappist monk.

One might, in any case, be uneasy about simulating an interview with a 'great man' (or great woman), still alive, or recently dead: one might scruple to put words into the mouth of one who is in a position to disown them – or whose heirs and assigns are in such a position.

One does not have to read far in the pages of Flora Thompson's *Lark Rise* to be sure that she would have been delighted to answer questions about herself, and her childhood in rural Oxfordshire. In every part of her autobiographical trilogy (*Lark Rise*, 1939, *Over to Candleford*, 1941, and *Candleford Green*, 1943 – issued in one volume as *Lark Rise to Candleford* in 1945) Flora Thompson is revealed as a lady who would not only have answered all one's questions patiently and graciously, she would have served tea and home-made scones besides.

Flora Thompson was not secretive, but she was modest. *Lark Rise* is autobiography (again, Penguin Books say so), but it purports to be the true story of an Oxfordshire hamlet, and of the young lives of Laura and her brother Edmund. It is not a novel, and it does not read like a novel. But Flora Thompson stands as far outside herself, for modesty's sake, as any autobiographer could be expected to do. She was discreet, and unshockable. When:

> *Laura, at about twelve years old, stumbled into a rickyard where a bull was in the act of justifying its existence, the sight did not warp her nature. She neither peeped from behind a rick, nor fled, horrified, across country; but merely thought in her old-fashioned way, 'Dear me! I had better slip quietly away before the men see me.' The bull was to her but a bull performing a necessary function if there was to be butter on the bread and bread and milk for breakfast, and she thought it quite natural that the men in attendance at such functions should prefer not to have women or little girls as spectators. They would have felt as they would have said, 'a bit okkard'. She just withdrew and went another way round without so much as a kink in her subconscious.*
>
> Penguin edition, p. 46

Much of the book is social history; there are the big house and the carriage folk, and there are the 'housen' with only one room downstairs, and that ill-furnished. The daughters went into service, the young men went to work in a town or to fight on Vimy Ridge, and the old listened to sermons about the 'rightness of the social order' that was passing even as they prayed. But it is Laura, with her good sense and sensitivity, who gives the book its personal touch, and whose self-depreciation wins our sympathy.

> *'Dibs' was a girls' game, played with five small, smooth pebbles, which had to be kept in the air at the same time and caught on the back of the hand. Laura, who was clumsy with her hands, never mastered this game; nor could she play marbles or spin tops or catch balls, or play hopscotch. She was by common consent 'a duffer'. Skipping and running were her only accomplishments.*

She is too hard on herself: she could read – and she did read, endlessly; and she could write, more enthrallingly than most.

Interview Flora Thompson as if for a modern magazine or newspaper. Ask her what she thought of the coming of the motor-car, and of the impact of wars, and of royal deaths. Ask her whether she would have preferred to live in a city – and answer in ways that are consistent with what she *does* have to say in *Lark Rise*.

(Such an approach could be made to any similar autobiographical work. 'Miss Read' of *Village School* and Robert Roberts of *A Ragged Schooling* would interview well. So would Sid Chaplin of *The Day of the Sardine*, Richard Wright of *Black Boy* and Leslie Thomas of *This Time Next Week*.)

5 Publisher's blurb

A title generally tells us something about the contents of a book. *Lark Rise to Candleford* tells us rather little, but the front cover of the 1970s Penguin Modern Classics edition framed a detail from *Country Scene*, a painting by Helen Allingham of a little girl standing at the garden gate of a half-timbered cottage, watching a boy loaded with hay. The house and garden are overspread with vegetation, and the girl stands and stares wistfully. The effect is of rusticity and of remoteness in time.

Because this is a Penguin book, we know that we shall learn more about the book by reading the rear cover. There, in 40 words out of a total 140, we are told that *Lark Rise . . .* is

> . . . a record in which she (Flora Thompson) brilliantly engraves the fast-dissolving England of peasant, yeoman and craftsman, and tints her picture with the cheerful courage and the rare pleasures that marked a self-sufficient world of work and poverty.
>
> Penguin edition, rear cover

One cannot say much in 140 words. Most of us want to know something of what a book is 'about' – and, perhaps, something of the author – before we commit ourselves to reading it.

Somehow, in the blurb, the publisher must reassure us that the book conforms to type: it is history, autobiography, social comment, novel, travelogue, or whatever. We want to know whether we shall be given data or humour (or both), figures or reminiscences (or neither). If we ask for bread, we shan't want a stone.

The blurb must 'sell' the book to us by an appeal to the familiar in familiar language. The writer of the blurb on the rear cover of Brian Friel's play *Translations* (see Chapter 2, page 35), cannot have been targeting a mass market when he described the Baile Beag 'scholars' as:

> a cross-section of the local community, from a semi-literate young farmer to an elderly polyglot autodidact . . .

Not only must a book fit some existing category, however; it must (it almost goes without saying) be somehow 'unique'. It must be the same, but different: it must attract the readers of the category of books that it fits, but it must be different from all the other books in that category.

I Know Why the Caged Bird Sings is the first volume in an autobiographical trilogy by Maya Angelou, a black American woman in her sixties. It is about being young and black – and a girl – in the Arkansas of the 1930s. It is about struggle. Now – as it seems to Ms Angelou – the young have given up the struggle, thinking the battle for black rights has been won:

> I know that many of us of another generation, established writers and so, are looked at almost as if we are relics.

The Guardian, 15 July 1988

Writing (recognition, an identity, love) did not come easily to Ms Angelou. She had to work at it, so she does not accept easy answers from those to whom it has come easy:

> Too many young Blacks, as far as I can see it, and young whites for that matter, have been told that if you just tell what you think, that is great writing. Well, that is not so, as we know.

The Guardian, 15 July 1988

Maya Angelou

She wonders what she fought for, when what she sees about her is:

> a temporary world with sit-coms where everything is resolved in twenty-seven minutes...

The Guardian, 15 July 1988

But she has not lost hope. 'Caged Bird', as she calls it, is an initiation into black 'inferiority' and personal tragedy; out of it (the blurb-writer says), 'her extraordinary sense of wholeness emerges'.

> *Another day was over. In the soft dark the cotton truck spilled the pickers out and roared out of the yard with a sound like a giant's fart. The workers stepped around in circles for a few seconds as if they had found themselves unexpectedly in an unfamiliar place. Their minds sagged.*
>
> *In the store the men's faces were the most painful to watch, but I seemed to have no choice. When they tried to smile to carry off their tiredness as if it was nothing, the body did nothing to help the mind's attempt to disguise. Their shoulders drooped even as they laughed, and when they put their hands on their hips in a show of jauntiness, the palms slipped the thighs as if the pants were waxed.*
>
> *'Evening, Sister Henderson. Well, back where we started, huh?'*
>
> *'Yes, sir, Brother Stewart. Back where you started, bless the Lord.'*
>
> *Momma could not take the smallest achievement for granted. People whose history and future were threatened each day by extinction considered that it was only by divine intervention that they were able to live at all.*

Virago paperback, p. 116

Maya Angelou was a victim of neglect, rape, discrimination, poverty and plain ignorance – but she lived, and *I Know Why the Caged Bird Sings* is the tale. Or the song.

Note
The above quotations from *The Guardian* are taken from *Writing Lives: Conversations between Women Writers*, Virago.

 If you had to write a publisher's blurb for Ms Angelou's book (a rather longer blurb than most), what would you say about it to suggest that it conforms to a certain type of literature? More significantly, what would you say about it to highlight its differentness? What could you say about the book that would 'sell' it?

6 A participant's journal

Maya Angelou's memories read with the immediacy of instant recall. Some people – even (or perhaps especially) quite elderly people – remember their childhood 'as if it was yesterday'. Laurie Lee did, Graham Greene did, and Flora Thompson did. It is likely, though, that they had kept a diary of some sort, or that they had recourse to letters or other memorabilia that served to set up associations in their minds. To one who writes a biography of someone not known personally – and even of someone who is – diaries and letters are useful, even necessary, raw materials.

The diaries of great public figures have been edited and published in their original form. Middleton Murry not only wrote a 'life' of his wife, Katherine Mansfield, he also published her letters and journal. Leonard Woolf published extracts from Virginia's *A Writer's Diary* (1953); and Arnold Bennett's *Journals* were edited in three volumes in 1932–3. Some writers (who live long enough) prefer to see their own journals through the press themselves.

Spender's Life Studies

John Bayley on a poet's flair for catching 'the turn of the true.'

Journals 1939–1983, by Stephen Spender (Faber, £15)
Collected Poems, 1928–1985, by Stephen Spender (Faber, £12.50, £4.95 paper)
The Oedipus Trilogy of Sophocles: a version by Stephen Spender (Faber, £12.50)

IN ENGLAND both politics and poetry seem to depend on personality more than they do elsewhere. Auden and Spender, legendary names of the late thirties, now seem to have settled into themselves — selves that are warm and homely and fallible and charming. Their writing speaks of themselves; why they are as they are and behave as they do, rather than of clashes and issues, romantic struggle and heroic ideology.

It is the importance of personality that makes these **Journals** so fascinating. Everyone in them comes alive on their own terms, for Spender has a Boswellian flair for giving the turn of the true to everyone he mentions, and also for taking himself interestedly, but not seriously.

The Guardian

Occasionally, writers have kept journals of particular episodes in their lives. Travel seems to be a particularly potent inducement to keeping a diary. The same Stephen Spender's *Learning Laughter* (1952), for example, is 'A Travel-Diary on Israel', and Aldous Huxley's *Jesting Pilate* (1926) is 'the diary of a journey'. Indeed, many a travel-book (such as Graham Greene's *Lawless Roads* on Liberia, and Auden's *Journey to a War* with Isherwood on China) is a diary in disguise.

Antony Sher kept a diary of sorts (dictated to a 'lovely lady' typist) when he played the title role in Shakespeare's *Richard III* at Stratford-upon-Avon in 1984. He called his record: *Year of the King*. (Would his journal have been studied as a coursework text if Sher had been a professional footballer instead of an actor – and an actor in a Shakespeare play, at that? It's a question worth asking.)

The first entry is headed: 'Barbican, August 1983, Summer'. He had played Molière in *Molière*, and was now playing Tartuffe in *Tartuffe*. That he might play Richard III in *Richard III* was suggested to him in an Italian restaurant on Monday 7 November of that year.

> *Over lunch, Bill offers me Richard III. Although I've been expecting it, my heart misses a beat.*
>
> Methuen edition, p. 20

He had been expecting it because he had been promised a 'Shakespeare biggy', and because three or four years had passed since Alan Howard's production of the play.

Sher is overpowered by the seemingly definitive interpretation of the part by Laurence Olivier, so he is determined that his will be a very different Richard. He reads about famous murderers of the past and present, he studies the pathology of physical deformities, and he observes patients at a spastics' work centre and a disabled games group – and all the time he sketches what he sees in stark black and white.

The elements fuse in a black-leather hunchback on crutches, like a 'bottled spider'.

Rehearsals began on Wednesday, 25 April 1984, and the play was performed before its first audience four hectic weeks later.

> Wednesday 23 May
> QUEEN MARGARET SCENE *All morning spent on this. Unravelling, disciplining, simplifying and, best of all,* cutting – *immediately makes it easier to play.*
>
> *One of the problems had been that the climax seems to be the confrontation between Margaret and Richard. Yet after this, Shakespeare has her cursing the others again. Most of this stuff gets cut. Pat loses a lot but takes it well and with good humour.*

As he's racing against time with the morning schedule, Bill says to her, 'Let's just try to get to your exit, Pat, get you off.'

She says, 'Yes please. I can imagine someone in the front row saying, "Dear oh dear, I thought she'd never go." '

She needn't worry. Her Margaret will be striking and original.

RUN-THROUGH OF ACT I *Still the most difficult Act for me. And the thought of having to do that opening speech in front of the Company for the first time . . . oh God. Just before we start, I feel the* fear, *like a raging distant storm. I turn my back on it.*

' "Now is the winter . . ." '

The run is thrilling. So many things fall into place for me. Richard's soliloquies and asides, which have seemed both bland and embarrassing in solus sessions, are actually enjoyable to do now. An audience at last – people to tell the story to. Get some encouraging laughs from the assembled cast and at other times the silences are palpable. (Contrary to popular belief in the profession, I feel that rehearsal laughs can be a useful guideline.)

Afterwards, Frances is very encouraging and Blessed does his wonderful machine-gun support: 'Bravo, 'kin marvellous, very exciting, very original, going to be sensational, 'kin terrific . . .' One or two other people pat my shoulder, compliment me on clarity and above all, speed.

If nothing else, mine will be the fastest Richard ever.

(p. 206)

But there was much else. There was a new, 'definitive' interpretation of the role, and there was the *Standard* Award for Best Actor of 1985. And there is a diary-and-sketchbook-in-one of an actor's tryst with a formidable part.

Sher gives us a stream-of-consciousness account of himself. We know him pretty well by the time he has finished dictating in his Chipping Campden cottage. But he introduces us to a number of his co-comedians and company retainers: Bill Alexander (producer), Pat Routledge (Queen Margaret), Bill Dudley (designer), Brian Blessed (Hastings), and many others.

You could take any part of the fourth chapter of the book (April–August 1984, pp. 155–249) and keep a journal in the name of any of these participants, perhaps spending most of your words on your impression of Sher's 'bottled spider'.

7 Debate

Virginia Woolf has been mentioned already once or twice in this book. She is best known as the author of nine novels, which include *The Voyage Out* (1915), *Mrs Dalloway* (1925), *To The Lighthouse* (1927) and *The Waves* (1931). But she also wrote much non-fiction: biographies, essays, tracts, letters (published by her husband after her death), and 'A Writer's Diary'. But perhaps her single most famous non-fiction work was an essay based on two lectures given by invitation to the fellows and undergraduates of two women's colleges in Cambridge, Newnham and Girton, in October 1928. The essay was called *A Room of One's Own*. It was published in 1929 and appeared under the Penguin imprint in 1945, four years after her death by drowning in the River Ouse. A photograph, and the rather terse tribute that accompanied it (opposite), were printed on the rear cover of that early Penguin edition.

We are over-inclined to think of Virginia Woolf as the privately educated daughter of an upper middle-class intellectual, who lived and breathed art and letters with upper middle-class intellectuals in Bloomsbury, and who wrote novels about the upper middle-class intellects of her family and friends. When we think of her as a *woman*, we think of her nervous condition, her insulation from the problems that faced most women, and her enigmatic end in the Ouse.

A Room of One's Own reveals her as a pioneer in what we now call the 'women's movement'. She neither ranted, nor did she campaign. Precisely because she did not share the problems of most women, she could not articulate those problems. At the

VIRGINIA WOOLF, who died in 1941, was the daughter of Sir Leslie Stephen, K.C.B., and the wife of Leonard Woolf.

Her first books were novels, and at the time of her death she had won a foremost place in English fiction, but she also ranks high among literary critics and essayists. Two collections of her essays, *The Common Reader* and *The Second Common Reader*, have been published by Penguin Books in their Pelican series; and her fantastic and beautiful novel *Orlando* has also appeared as a Penguin Book.

A Room of One's Own, Penguin edition rear cover

same time, as a sensitive and intelligent woman, she was better placed than most to question male-dominance in art, in letters, and in public affairs. Her thesis was – explicitly – that 'a woman must have money and a room of her own if she is to write fiction'. Implicitly, however, Virginia Woolf's real objective was room for a woman in history.

> By no possible means could middle-class women with nothing but brains and character at their command have taken part in any one of the great movements which, brought together, consitute the historian's view of the past. Nor shall we find her in any collection of anecdotes. Aubrey hardly mentions her. She never writes her own life and scarcely keeps a diary; there are only a handful of her letters in existence. She left no plays or poems by which we can judge her. What one wants, I thought – and why does not some brilliant student at Newnham or Girton supply

Alternative English

> it? – is a mass of information; at what age did she marry; how many children had she as a rule; what was her house like; had she a room to herself; did she do the cooking; would she be likely to have a servant? All these facts lie somewhere, presumably, in parish-registers and account books; the life of the average Elizabethan woman must be scattered about somewhere, could one collect it, and make a book of it (. . .)
>
> Here I am asking why women did not write poetry in the Elizabethan age, and I am not sure how they were educated; whether they were taught to write; whether they had sitting rooms to themselves; how many women had children before they were twenty-one; what, in short, they did from eight in the morning till eight at night. They had no money, evidently; according to Professor Trevelyan they were married whether they liked it or not before they were out of the nursery, at fifteen or sixteen very likely. It would have been extremely odd, even upon this showing, had one of them suddenly written the plays of Shakespeare, I concluded, and I thought of that old gentleman, who is dead now, but was a bishop, I think, who declared that it was impossible for any woman, past, present, or to come, to have the genius of Shakespeare.

A chapter or two later, Virginia Woolf turned her attention from Elizabethan poetry to the Victorian novel. In that time, and in that genre, women writers would seem at last to have come into their own. Not so, Virginia Woolf explains: the woman novelist was confined within the narrow room left her by the man's-world values that continued to predominate, and that discounted hers.

> Since a novel has this correspondence to real life, its values are to some extent those of real life. But it is obvious that the values of women differ very often from the values which have been made by the other sex; naturally, this is so. Yet it is the masculine values that prevail. Speaking crudely, football and sport are 'important'; the worship of fashion, the buying of clothes 'trivial'. And these values are inevitably transferred from life to fiction. This is an important book, the critic assumes, because it deals with war. This is an insignificant book because it deals with the feelings of women in a drawing-room. A scene in a battle-field is more important than a scene in a shop – everywhere and much more subtly the difference of value persists.

 Respond to Virginia Woolf's arguments in debating fashion. Have the historians a distorted view of the past in their exclusion of women from 'the great movements'? How would the 'mass of information' of which she speaks affect our view of women's contribution to 'history'?

Did the 'old gentleman', the bishop, have a point? Why do 'masculine values' prevail? If they have done in the past, do they now?

Will even a 'difference of value' persist in the future, do you think? You might lay out your argument in the form of a debating speech, designed to win a vote.

8 A personal view

> ... when a subject is highly controversial – and any question about sex is that – one cannot hope to tell the truth.

By this controversial remark, Virginia Woolf meant that no comment about sex can be absolutely and objectively true. Apart from any other reason for subjectivity in this context is the fact that the commentator must be male or female – he or she cannot be both, therefore he or she can never see the subject from both points of view.

A debate is by definition a controversy (where there is only one point of view, there is no debate), but a debater would not normally argue from personal experience, any more than would a barrister in a court of law.

It is the premiss of this book that students of 16–19 years of age should not be expected to engage in 'literary criticism' of the conventional kind because they cannot have read enough to be able to make the comparisons that are the very stuff of criticism. But students of 16–19 might be expected to have read a good deal of literature of a sort that would not normally be subject to 'literary' criticism, but which might well be subject to much adult criticism in the common sense of this word. I refer to comics, to young people's magazines, and to adventure and romantic fiction.

Ever since George Orwell wrote his celebrated essay on 'Boys' Weeklies' in 1944, young people's 'pulp' fiction has been a fit subject for investigation by the nostalgic and censorious – and well-intentioned – among journalists, populist academics and social scientists. One (mostly level-headed) study was made by Bob Dixon and published by Pluto Press under the title: *Catching Them Young: Political Ideas in Children's Fiction*. In his first chapter, he deplores the gender stereotyping to be found in girls' and boys' comics:

> *The extracts from this strip* (Mandy) *give a good idea of the emotional atmosphere of the greater part of the strips in these comics. It's not only the squalid sentimentality which gives rise to concern but the fact that girls are so frequently seen to be acted upon, rather than acting, to be in passive, powerless situations where all they seem to be able to do is suffer, to the point of masochism (...)*

> *The whole psychological syndrome is both interesting and disturbing. It can clearly be related to the role which women have fallen into over a very long period in our society. The tendency is for them to have no autonomy, to speak of, to act as adjuncts to their husbands and to live for and through husbands and children. This, in turn, accounts for the emptiness felt by many women – especially when their families have grown up – and the possessiveness mothers exert over their children, of whatever age, and the havoc this causes. We can see it all happening in comics.*
>
> Pluto Press edition, p. 25

Dixon goes on to examine magazines for teenage girls. In these:

> *. . . the stress is, overwhelmingly, on fashion and cosmetics, how to package oneself for the romance market, how to meet boys, how to conduct oneself on dates (but the odd horse still keeps coming in here and there), how to behave – what to do – to be accepted and sought after.*
>
> (p. 35)

Next, it's the turn of the boys' comics to be dissected:

> *. . . it's possible to distinguish three major preoccupations in boys' comics. These are the menace, the superman or power theme, and war. Even these can be further reduced to a preoccupation with the conflict between a clearly-distinguished 'good' and a just as obviously delineated 'evil', resulting in 'goodies' and 'baddies' who can be readily identified as such from the drawings. You just have to look at their faces.*
>
> (p. 36)

Advertisements in boys' comics range from stamp collecting, conjuring and practical jokes of the 'amaze your friends' variety to an obvious mirroring of the fictional content. Where there's such a stress on physical strength, we naturally find advertisements for body-building courses. Charles Atlas often comes in, as if on cue, wanting to prove that 'you too can have a body like [his]!' though you don't have to have one like his. You can 'Just choose the body you want and post the coupon'. Where there's such emphasis (. . .) on law and order and war, we naturally find many advertisements for war toys and models as well as heavy recruitment campaigns for the police and armed forces. The latter stress the travel, adventure and learn-a-trade aspects, not, it need hardly be said, the killing.

(p. 50)

 Did you read comics or magazines of this sort? (Do you still?) If so, consider yourself an expert – you will know more about such things than the average adult, just by being a lot closer.

Do you think you 'learned' anything from what you read? Did you realise you were being socialised into 'masochism' or 'macho-ism'? Are children likely to be influenced, for good or ill, by the comics they read? Base considered opinions on your own reading history.

Alternatively, you could subject what you read now to such a critical evaluation. If you read women's magazines, for example, you could take as a point of departure for your analysis Chapter 5, 'Women's Magazine Fiction: Love Ideology for the Dependent Woman', in *Romantic Love and Society: Its Place in the Modern World* by Jacqueline Sarsby (Penguin Books, 1983).

FIVE

The 'long' coursework essay

What are the requirements?

The examining boards modify their syllabuses with some frequency. In recent years, with the advent of GCSE and AS Level courses (and TVEI and modularity and the National Curriculum), the pace of change has quickened. But it is teachers (to say nothing of their students) in the schools and colleges who have pressed for coursework syllabuses in English, and the coursework element has grown markedly as a proportion of each of these syllabuses, as the years have passed.

Most of the pieces of coursework required by the boards will call for 'engagement' with just one text at a time. Such pieces are expected to be 800–1,200 words in length (AEB A and AS Level), or between 1,000 and 2,000 words (London 170, Paper 4C), or up to 2,000 words (JMB Syllabus C). The London Board does not require any one of its essays to be longer than others, but the JMB and AEB do. The former calls for one piece, under the heading 'Wide Reading', to be of approximately 2,500 words (though two pieces, each of 1,500 words, can be submitted as an alternative), and, it is said, this 'long' piece 'must deal with more than one book'. This requirement obtains at both A and AS examinations.

The AEB A Level syllabus (660) contains the following stipulation:

> The coursework will (. . .) include one extended essay of about 3,000 words on a broader basis than a single text (. . .) The extended essay may arise from the study of a prescribed text or a book chosen for coursework, but should not be exclusively concerned with this book.

Finally, the Cambridge Board (UCLES) A Level and AS Level syllabuses allow for – but do not prescribe – a 'sustained piece of work/project/individual study' as one component in a folder of between five and eight pieces of work having an overall total of no more than 7,500 words. Thus the length of the 'sustained piece of work' will depend upon the length of each of the other four, five, six or seven pieces, but it is likely to be of between 2,000 and 4,000 words.

The two fundamental differences between the 'long' ('extended' or 'sustained') essay and 'short' essays, therefore, are:

1 it will be between one and a half to three times as long as a normal essay;

2 it will (probably) deal with two or more texts.

A third difference may be that, whereas teachers choose the coursework texts (in light of what they know, what they find will 'teach well' and what is inexpensive or – better still – in stock), students will be given discretion to choose the texts on which their long essays will be based for themselves.

If candidates are encouraged, in all the pieces of coursework, to speak in a 'personal and individual voice', this encouragement is still stronger in respect of the long essay.

The Cambridge Board warns against the setting of too high a *minimum* number of words for the 'sustained' essay, since this

> ...leads candidates into mechanical and uncritical presentation of historical, biographical, geographical, social background material, the sole function of which is to achieve the minimum word limit.

Doubtless, all the other boards would second this remonstrance. They all value attention to *text* above excursions into *context*.

Secondary sources of any sort are looked upon with suspicion, for fear that students will plagiarise 'good' criticism and – worse – transcribe or mimic 'bad' criticism (by which they would mean revision notes of the mass-market kind). The Cambridge Board insists that critical works be 'properly acknowledged, with footnotes and bibliographies appended', and, again, other boards would wholeheartedly agree.

The only other major, stated claim is (in the words of the AEB Chief Examiner) that there are clear advantages to choosing 'a well delimited topic, close to the real interests of the student'. Just as the title of a novel or play or poem is a guide to what it is 'about', so the title of an essay determines what it *can* – even *must* – be about. The choice of essay title is a crucial matter for negotiation between student and teacher, therefore no suggestion made below is in any sense a short cut. The ideas put forward for 'long-essay' subjects are intended to stimulate students' own ideas, give them some guidance as to the sort of title that is likely to be acceptable and so brief them in negotiation with their course-teacher. A student informed is a student forearmed.

Above all, you the student must want to write the essay. You must be sufficiently gripped by what you have read to want to talk about it, explore the ideas and answer some of the questions that have been raised in *your* mind. The writing must have challenged you somehow. It must have held you in such a way that you will write about it 'effectively, and appropriately', and in all the other adverbial ways referred to in the course objectives.

Examiners are looking for signs of excitement, as well as of critical understanding. For all the talk (above) of hundreds and thousands, they are not counting words. You should not be counting words either.

What line might one take?

The AEB's Syllabus 660 makes three quite concrete suggestions as to what the extended essay might be 'about'.

> The subject may be a genre within a period (e.g. the treatment of the Crucifixion in medieval plays); a theme (comparison of 'Utopias'); several works by one writer (e.g. Graham Greene's novels with tropical settings).

Of the 57 long essay titles chosen by students in four English sets in one sixth-form college (all of them acceptable to the Moderator):

(Category 1)   6 students wrote about a 'genre within a period';

(Category 2)   17 students wrote about a 'theme'; and

(Category 3)   34 students wrote about 'several works by one writer'.

In fact the three categories are not hard and fast. Very few essays in the third category focused on the writers themselves, as these two titles did:

> 'A study of the development of Ted Hughes's poetry from *The Hawk in the Rain* to *What is the Truth?*'

> 'Evelyn Waugh's development from comedy to tragedy: *Decline and Fall, A Handful of Dust,* and *Brideshead Revisited.*'

Most essays about writers fastened on a single theme or preoccupation identifiable in (two or three examples of) their work, as these essays did:

> 'Hardy's treatment of three different women: Tess, Eustacia, Bathsheba.'

> ' "I am interested in how people treat each other. There's obviously a huge male/female rift in many of my plays." A discussion of *Absent Friends, A Chorus of Disapproval,* and *Confusions* in the light of Ayckbourn's own comment.'

'Chaucer's presentation of love and marriage in "The Clerk's Tale", "The Merchant's Tale", and "The Franklin's Tale".'

Perhaps the clearest examples of Category 1 titles of the six so delineated were these two:

'The changing mood of Irish poetry before, during and after the 1916 Rebellion, with particular reference to Yeats.'

'Faith and fiction: *Jude the Obscure* by Thomas Hardy, and *The Way of All Flesh* by Samuel Butler.'

BBC Radio frequently writes essays in sound of the Category 1 type. Eugene O'Neill and Edward Albee are paired, though, rather in space than in time.

The playman cometh

R3 Eugene O'Neill, widely regarded as the greatest playwright America has ever produced and so far the only one to be awarded the Nobel Prize for Literature, was born 100 years ago next week.

Radio 3 will be celebrating the centenary with some of his greatest plays but this week the writer is put into timely perspective in **Remembering O'Neill** (Wednesday 9.25pm). In a rare interview with Edward Albee, who was once seen as O'Neill's heir, theatre critic Benedict Nightingale, explores O'Neill's prolific output and assesses his contemporary standing. The domestic agonies of Albee's *Who's Afraid of Virginia Woolf?* are generally thought to have been influenced by O'Neill.

'It seemed a good idea to talk to a leading American playwright of today about this giant of the creative past,' says Benedict. 'I was a little nervous that it might prove a difficult interview but Albee, who is hoping that his own new play will open in both New York and London in December, was only too happy to talk.'

O'Neill's often tragic and tortured life has been well documented, not least in his hauntingly autobiographical *Long Day's Journey into Night* which depicted his father, a famous actor, as a miserly old ham, his mother as a 'dope fiend' (O'Neill's phrase), his brother as a flamboyant alcoholic and the playwright himself as a tubercular failure.

Radio Times

Arthur Miller's *All My Sons* could have been added, leading to an essay written under the title: ' "Domestic agonies" in the plays of three Americans: O'Neill, Albee and Miller.'

Place linked at least two twentieth-century novels in a *Radio Times* feature about the actor Peter McEnery: Arnold Bennett's *The Old Wives' Tale*, and D. H. Lawrence's *Sons and Lovers*. McEnery, himself a Midlander, compares the two novelists as Midlands writers. But it is on the grounds of his 'compassion' and his 'remarkable understanding of love and of women' that Bennett is adjudged to come out on top.

> **Peter's back to the Potteries**
>
> **R4** Peter McEnery found television fame more than ten years ago through Arnold Bennett's *Clayhanger*, and this week radio happily reunites him with the author in the new classic serial, **The Old Wives' Tale** (Friday 3.00), an adaptation of one of Bennett's most successful novels. Edwin Clayhanger won Peter a heart-throb following but he doubts if Gerald Scales, the man he plays in the new serial, will do the same.
>
> *The Old Wives' Tale* chronicles the lives of two sisters – Gerald will marry one of them. 'He's a small-time commercial traveller who cuts a dash with the ladies – a sharp lad with an eye for the main chance,' says Peter. 'I can't say I like him much but I do like going back to Bennett. I'm a Midlander myself – though not from the Five Towns – and his books recall stories my father told me about his boyhood.'
>
> Peter says he prefers Bennett's writing to that of his Midlands contemporary D. H. Lawrence. 'I always wanted to appear in *Sons and Lovers* and finally did it on radio, but I'm more impressed by Bennett's compassion. For a man who was a virgin until he was 40 he had a remarkable understanding of love and of women.'
>
> David Gillard, *Radio Times*, 23–29 January 1988

Attitudes towards women supplied the theme for a number of the 17 Category 2 essays:

> 'Male attitudes to women as shown in *The French Lieutenant's Woman* and *Tess of the D'Urbervilles*.'

for instance, and:

> 'A comparison of two heroines: Cathy in *Wuthering Heights* by E. Brontë, and Jane in *Jane Eyre* by C. Brontë.'

South Africa is a long way from the English Midlands. From what David Gillard says of Christopher Hope's novel, *White Boy Running* (*Radio Times*, 1–7 October 1988), it could fitly be paired with *Middlepost* by Antony Sher, to which reference has already been made: 'Insights by *émigrés* [perhaps]: novels about South Africa by Christopher Hope and Antony Sher.' If the 'childhood' sections of the Hope and the Lithuanian sections of the Sher were omitted, one might add the works of Alan Paton or Nadine Gordimer to the analysis – both of them, as it were, internal exiles in South Africa.

India is another country much visited by twentieth-century novelists: E. M. Forster of course, John Masters, J. G. Farrell, Paul Scott – and that's before starting on writers for whom India has been home: Anita Desai, R. Prawer Jhabvala, and R. K. Narayan.

Among the most imaginative Category 2 titles submitted by the 17 students were these three:

> ' "No rings attached" – the treatment of unmarried mothers in three twentieth-century novels: *The L-shaped Room* (Lynn Reid Banks), *The Millstone* (Margaret Drabble) and *Emmeline* (Judith Rossner).'

'The struggles of the individual in three future worlds: Orwell's *Nineteen Eighty-Four*, Margaret Atwood's *Handmaid's Tale* and *Riddley Walker* by Russell Hoban.'

'The problem of old age and senility as seen in William Trevor's *The Old Boys*, Susan Hill's *Gentlemen and Ladies*, and Barbara Pym's *Quartet in Autumn*.'

Out of South Africa

Questioning: Christopher Hope

R4 Last year the South African born, award-winning novelist Christopher Hope returned to his troubled homeland for the first time in 12 years for what he calls 'a venture into my own interior'. The result was his new book *White Boy Running* (Secker and Warburg, £10.95), a look back to his childhood but also a raw, contemporary assessment of a country in which, he says, 'movement gives the illusion of progress'. On Monday it begins a ten-part adaptation as **A Book at Bedtime** (10.15pm).

Actor and writer Jack Klaff, who reads *White Boy Running* and also read Hope's *The Hottentot Room* for *Bedtime*, is another self-imposed South African exile; he settled in Britain 15 years ago and has never been back. 'We're both children of apartheid. There's a number of similarities between my experiences and Christopher's,' he says.

Hope's visit coincided with the all-white election of May 1987 and his book, says Jack, 'is a very clear and up-to-date picture of what's going on. Yes, it's an indictment but it's a book that asks questions rather than points fingers.' Jack – recently heard on radio in *Pelléas and Mélisande* and seen on BBC1 last year as Rawdon Crawley in *Vanity Fair* – has himself often written about his homeland. His radio play *Madam's Good Girl* was set in South Africa, as was his Channel Four history of events at the time of the Sharpeville massacre (he played all the parts), *Nagging Doubt*.

David Gillard, *Radio Times*, 1–7 October 1988

Perhaps it is that students are accustomed to writing about the work of one author rather than on a theme that provoked twice as many Category 3 as opposed to Category 2 essay titles; or perhaps it is that the media tend to focus on one author at a time – understandably; or perhaps it is simply that there really is more that unites two or three works by one author, under one heading, than there is in two or three works by two or three authors. The likelihood is, in fact, that it will be *one* work that you *like* that suggests to you what you might write about. What is more natural than that you should compare or contrast that work with another by the same author? When BBC Television trained its cameras on the work of the novelist Fay Weldon, the theme that emerged was 'the nature of evil'.

Fay's eye on evil

'In discussions of this kind, people tend to polarise themselves,' says playwright and author Fay Weldon. The discussion in question – seen in **Thinking Aloud** on BBC2 on Thursday – is about the nature of evil, on which Fay (whose *Life and Loves of a She Devil* caused such a stir when it was first shown on BBC2 last year) is something of an expert.

'I tend to see evil as a force,' Fay continues. 'When people are malicious or go through patches of being destructive, it's a kind of possession by demons. I believe in demons rather than the devil.'

Fay is currently working on a new TV mini-series, *Greenfingers*, in which, she says, the struggle between good and evil is central. 'It explores the worlds of the organic and the inorganic – roses and nuclear power if you like – which are always in a state of conflict.'

Nicki Household, 'Upfront', *Radio Times*, 12–18 December 1987

Fay Weldon's work raised other questions in the mind of one of the Category 3 students:

> 'Is Fay Weldon a serious writer? Does she like women? A consideration of *Life and Loves of a She Devil, Praxis, The President's Child* and some short stories.'

That was an ambitious – perhaps over-ambitious – title, involving as it did three titles and more.

On the whole, two titles (especially if they are two lengthy novels) are probably enough. Two collections of poems or short stories would yield plenty of material too, but one might explore themes in three plays, or three novellas – there are no rules in this connection. It matters only that one has as much material as one needs – and no more than one needs – for an investigation in some depth and breadth that makes comparisons and draws contrasts, that is interested and thoughtful, and that will interest and provoke thought.

Sue Summers interviewed Harold Pinter when his new 25-minute play, *Mountain Language*, was performed for the first time at the National Theatre. Reviewers seemed to notice, as if for the first time, that Pinter is a political animal.

Harold Pinter, whose plays have often dealt with powerlessness, tells **Sue Summers** about his obsession with the state of Britain

Harold Pinter's latest political act, the formation of a literary discussion group to counter the ideas of Mrs Thatcher, was the subject of more newspaper column inches than the average South American revolution. His first political act went unremarked by everyone except his parents, the Army and Moishe Wernick.

It was 1948 and the 18-year-old Pinter refused to be called up for military service, on the grounds that he was a conscientious objector. 'I disassociated myself from preparations for another war,' he says. 'It seemed to me that since the war which had cost millions and millions of lives had just finished, this Cold War stuff was crap.' The future playwright conducted his own defence at two civil trials and two tribunals in Fulham Town Hall, which he attended with his toothbrush in his pocket, fully expecting to go to prison for six months.

At the second tribunal, Pinter produced a character witness — Moishe Wernick, a friend of his own age from Hackney Downs Grammar School. 'I know Harold, and you don't,' Moishe told the assembly. 'He's very obstinate. If he says he won't do it, he won't.'

Harold Pinter tells the story to illustrate that politics is not something he has discovered in middle-age. 'It could even be said my early plays like *The Birthday Party* and *The Dumb Waiter* were political in a way,' he says. 'But they were sort of metaphors.' In the past 10 years, however, politics has become one of his major concerns, and at 6.15pm on Thursday at the première of *Mountain Language* — his first new play since the short work *One for the Road* four years ago — audiences at the National Theatre will see him attempting political theatre of a far more direct kind.

The Independent, 18 October 1988

It is difficult to be dispassionate about Pinter. His plays either take you, or leave you. The student who wrote an essay having the following title (and who investigated no fewer than four of Pinter's plays) was very taken by them:

> ' "People fall back on anything they can lay their hands on, verbally, to keep away from the danger of knowing, and of being known." (Pinter) A consideration of *The Caretaker, The Dumb Waiter, The Room* and *The Birthday Party*.'

The student had read *The Caretaker* and seen a video of *The Birthday Party*, and she was taken by the idea of 'knowing, and of being known' and of language – not as a failure of communication, but as a refusal to communicate. She might easily, and equally, have been taken by the idea of power and of powerlessness. The same works will take different people in different ways.

Among other valid, thoughtful, interested, interesting essays in the third category were these three:

> 'Laurens Van Der Post's attitude to other races and peoples as expressed in his novels *The Seed and the Sower* and *A Far-Off Place*, and in other writings: *The Night of the New Moon, Journey into Russia* and *The Lost World of the Kalahari.*'

> ' "Not waving but drowning": the search for a reason to live in Stevie Smith's novels: *Novel on Yellow Paper, Over the Frontier, The Holiday.*'

And after these multi-word, multi-work fiction and non-fiction prose-focused essays, a no-nonsense, briskly-worded, verse-focused title:

> 'Pessimism in the poetry of Thomas Hardy.'

How might one write the essay?

The interest that will set the juice of an idea flowing will be in a genre (ballad, revenge tragedy, science fiction), a period (Jacobean England, the Industrial Revolution, the Second World War), a theme (religious doubt, black consciousness, the American dream), an author or a book. On balance, as we have seen, it is most likely to be a book. This may then, in turn, point the student in the direction of another book by the same author, or to a book on the same theme by another author.

I shall use as the model for this section the example of an essay written about the 'angry young men' of the 1950s. The essay itself was unexceptional (it was awarded a grade C), but the approach that the student took – let us call her Tania – is one that you could adopt yourself to advantage.

Tania saw a fragment of John Osborne's play *Look Back in Anger* performed at her school by a small touring theatre company. An actor referred to John Osborne as an 'angry young man', and mentioned the novelists John Wain and Kingsley Amis as the writers of 'angry young man' novels. Tania had heard of these writers, but she could not have named any of their books.

The 'long' coursework essay

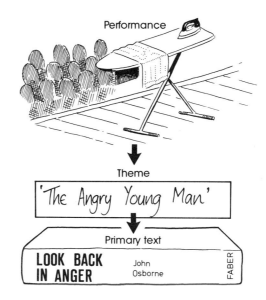

Having read the play, she could tell Jimmy Porter was angry. His anger is of the sort that bites people's heads off – even people he plainly loves. And it was obvious what it was he was angry about – his wife's world: 'all home-made cakes and croquet, bright ideas, bright uniforms . . . crisp linen, the smell of starch', the church, in which 'people are cut right off from the ugly problems of the twentieth century . . .', and anything and everything that (like Salinger's Holden Caulfield) he thinks is 'phoney'. Tania could tell Jimmy was angry: his anger was appalling, relentless, sadistic. He boasted of his anger ('I learnt at an early age what it was to be angry'), and his suffering was almost religious – angrier-than-thou ('I knew more about – love . . . betrayal . . . and death, when I was ten years old than you will probably ever know all your life') – so that when he said: 'I rage, and shout my head off, and everyone thinks "poor chap" or "what an objectionable young man!"' Tania quite agreed with everyone – except that she would have used a stronger word than 'objectionable'.

The play provoked a number of questions, which Tania wrote down:

1   Where did all Jimmy Porter's anger come from?

2   What was it directed against?

3   Were Jimmy Porter and John Osborne one and the same?

4   Who were the other 'angry young men'?

5   Were they all from a similar background?

6   Were they all angry about the same thing?

7   What became of these 'angry young men'?

8   How long did the 'angry young man' movement last?

These might not have been the only questions she could have asked – and they might not have been the best ones – but in asking questions of some kind Tania ruled a clear line of enquiry. [The already quoted AEB Chief Examiner wrote: 'There is a greater tendency (than in short essays) for candidates to rely more on "re-telling the story" of their chosen texts, unless clear lines of argument are established at an early stage . . .'] She knew what she was looking for in whatever other novels or plays she might read.

But what else should she read? How many 'angry young men' were there? Which of the books by John Wain and Kingsley Amis were 'angry young men' books? Were there others, more significant than theirs?

It was at this point that Tania went to the school library to look up 'Angry Young Man', 'Osborne', 'Wain' and 'Amis' in the reference section. She could have asked her course-teacher for suggestions, but Tania was the sort who feared to make a fool of herself in a display of ignorance. She preferred to find out something on her own first, and then seek confirmation that she had chosen wisely.

She would have learnt enough to start her off in a good encyclopaedia, but she found a number of books on the reference shelves of more obvious use:

The Concise Cambridge History of English Literature
   (George Sampson, Cambridge University Press, 3rd edn., 1970)

Longman Companion to Twentieth-Century Literature
   (A. C. Ward, Longman, 1970)

Twentieth-Century Writing: A Reader's Guide to Contemporary Literature
   (Ed. Kenneth Richardson, Newnes, 1969)

The Penguin Companion to Literature – 1 British and Commonwealth Literature
   (Ed. David Daiches, Penguin Books, 1971)

The Reader's Encyclopaedia
   (William Rose Benet, A. & C. Black, 3rd edn., 1988)

The Concise Oxford Dictionary of English Literature
   (Dorothy Eagle, OUP, 2nd edn., 1970)

Tania looked up 'Angry Young Men' in *The Reader's Encyclopaedia* and read the following: the label was

> ... applied to an unaffiliated group of English writers. Taken from the title of Leslie Allen Paul's autobiography *Angry Young Man* (1951) the term became widely used in connection with the kind of bitter dissidence expressed in John Osborne's play *Look Back in Anger*. The so-called Angry Young Men of British letters voiced their suspicion and resentment of the static English Establishment – its culture, manners, snobbism, and hypocrisy – chiefly through the novel and drama. Also identified with the group were the novelists Kingsley AMIS, Colin WILSON, John WAIN, and Alan SILLITOE, and the playwright Arnold WESKER.

Amis and Wain were there. 'Bitter dissidence' rang true, but Tania was unsure what to make of the 'static English Establishment'. Surely there must have been more to the anger of Osborne and Company than mere class envy? Tania looked up 'Angry Young Men' in the *Longman Companion*. Following the credit given to Leslie Paul and John Osborne, Tania read this paragraph:

> The other writers brought under this label, usually in spite of their own protests, included Kingsley *Amis, John *Wain, and John *Braine. In so far as there was a group anger it arose largely among those of working-class parentage who, having received university education from the state, found themselves thereafter socially stateless, out of contact and frequently out of sympathy with their family environment, yet unqualified by upbringing and temperament to be at ease on a different social level.

'Social misfits' A. C. Ward called them – a description that seemed to fit Jimmy Porter to a tee. According to Ward, the Angry Young Men were working class; they had been to university, and had found themselves in a social limbo, rejected alike by the class from which they had risen and by the class to which they aspired. They were angry because they had been thwarted. Here were the beginnings of an answer to Tania's question one. The entry under 'John Osborne' in *Twentieth-Century Writing* supplied something of an answer to her question three:

> At the time of the first performance, Osborne was in his late twenties. Like Jimmy Porter, the play's hero, he had come from a working-class background (...) In all of Osborne's plays there is a central protagonist, in whose speeches is to be heard the voice of Osborne himself. Jimmy's anger is substantially Osborne's anger – anger that, amongst other things, England's much vaunted social revolution of 1945–51, had changed so little.

What was this social revolution? A glance at the *Penguin Chronology of the Modern World*, farther along the shelf, was enough to remind Tania that 1945–51 were the years of the post-war Labour government of Clement Attlee. The Bank of England, the mines, the railways were nationalised; family allowances were introduced; the National Insurance and National Health Acts were passed and the Butler Education Act was implemented; Eire and India were given their independence; and all Commonwealth citizens were given British subject status. They were brave years, when many promises were made. Richard Hoggart (in *The Uses of Literacy*) called this brave new world a 'meritocracy': the deserving and the hard-working class would climb the ladder of the school system from the back street to the corridors of power.

By the 1950s, when the Conservatives under Churchill's leadership were back in power, it seemed to many young men – who thought themselves deserving – that nothing had changed, and that promises had been broken.

Tania read the brief biographies of Kingsley Amis, John Wain, John Braine and Alan Sillitoe in the *Penguin Companion*. She discovered thus that Dixon in Amis's *Lucky Jim* and Charles Lumley in Wain's *Hurry on Down* were both graduates, as Osborne's Jimmy Porter was. John Braine's Joe Lampton (in *Room at the Top*) and Alan Sillitoe's Arthur Seaton (in *Saturday Night and Sunday Morning*) were not. They were young men on the make, pleasure-seekers – not anti-establishment intellectuals or social-political idealists. This made them 'angry young men' of a different sort. Would it be better to write about the similarities of Wain's and Amis's heroes to John Osborne's; or to write about the dissimilarities to him of Braine's and Sillitoe's working-class anti-heroes?

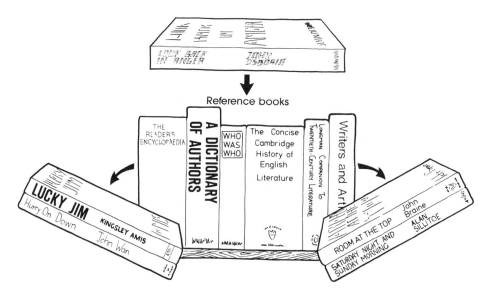

Tania inclined to the former view. Osborne had not been to university as Amis and Wain had (and Braine and Sillitoe had not), but she decided – wisely – that her essay must be about the books, and the characters in the books, not about the authors. Then she discovered that *Lucky Jim* and *Hurry on Down* were in the school library whilst the Braine and Sillitoe novels were not. This finding went a third of the way to confirming Tania's inclination, her teacher's approval went the second third, and a dip into *Hurry on Down* took her the rest of the way.

> *Dressed once more in the uniform of the class he had renounced, he surveyed himself critically in Betty's looking-glass. Apart from the fact that his frame had broadened, giving him something of the characteristic heavy-shouldered carriage of the manual worker, he still looked much the same. A cheap haircut had left him with an ugly matchstick-length crop, but that was the only class badge he was wearing, and it was not a conspicuous one.*
>
> *Thus equipped for a raid into enemy territory, he pushed through the swing doors of the town's Grand Hotel at dinner-time, determined to live at the rate of a thousand a year for the next few hours. Although he had, on occasions, cleaned the hotel's windows, no one recognised him; nor did he feel any fear that they would . . .*
>
> Penguin edition, p. 73

Charles Lumley, graduate, was a window-cleaner, just as Jimmy Porter, graduate, kept a sweet-stall. There was the same sensitivity to 'class' as in Osborne's play, and Charles Lumley's 'raid into enemy territory' reminded Tania of the 'raids on the enemy in W1, SW1, SW3, and W8', when Hugh, Jimmy and Alison (their 'hostage') gatecrashed parties at the town-houses of the smart set.

Tania decided that she would read *Hurry on Down* first, because it was published first (in 1953), and then *Lucky Jim*, published in the following year. Now that she had chosen these two books (and not the Braine and Sillitoe novels), she decided that she would be looking for similarities to the Osborne and not dissimilarities. If the point of the essay was to throw light on a common theme, this seemed the more reasonable line to take.

Now Tania was ready to submit a title, worded tightly enough to keep the body of the essay slim, but loosely enough to give her some room for manoeuvre:

> 'Three Angry Young Men (in works by Osborne, Amis and Wain) and the post-war Establishment.'

Tania looked back at the eight questions she had asked herself (see pages 125–6). She had worked out answers of sorts to questions 1 and 3 (where did all Jimmy Porter's anger come from, and were Jimmy Porter and John Osborne one and the same); and she had answered question 4 (who were the other 'angry young men') by choosing Amis and Wain from among the six names mentioned in the reference books. She decided to incorporate what she had learnt (from the *Penguin Chronology* and from GCSE history and a glance at a popular history of the period) about the welfare-state optimism of the 1940s and the disillusionment of the social-climbers in the 1950s in a brief introduction.

It is almost always worth devoting your first few paragraphs to putting your *primary text* (the Osborne in this case) into its historical context – and perhaps to explaining why you chose to study it.

Tania accepted K. R. Robinson's assertion (in his entry on John Osborne, in *Twentieth-Century Writing*) that 'Jimmy's anger is substantially Osborne's anger'; and she would quote (and acknowledge) Robinson's words, at the beginning of her first major section. This section would deal with question 2: What was (Jimmy's anger) directed against?

Tania read *Hurry on Down* and *Lucky Jim* with a view to being able to answer her questions 5 and 6 (were the 'angry young men' from similar backgrounds and were they all angry about the same things). She would be principally concerned with the characters – Jimmy Porter, Charles Lumley and Jim Dixon – not with their creators. But another question did occur to Tania at this point: How far (in effect) were Lumley and Wain one and the same? And Amis and Dixon? Did the three writers approve of their creatures? Were they 'baddies' or 'goodies', and did they 'win' or 'lose'? Were Porter and company heroes, or anti-heroes?

The essay was beginning to take shape:

Introduction	From high hopes to disillusionment. The genesis of the anti-Establishment 'anger' among young graduates.
Section 1	The objects of Jimmy Porter's anger: (a) the 'hypocrisy' of the Church in its support of the H-Bomb, and of 'class distinctions' (the 'Bishop of Bromley' passage, Faber edition, p. 13) (b) the dreariness of living in 'the American age' (p. 17) (c) the 'plundering' upper middle class (p. 20) and so on
Section 2	The reason for choosing Wain's and Amis's novels. A brief note about the background of these two writers.
Section 3	What were Charles Lumley and Jim Dixon angry about? (a) The butts of Charles Lumley's anger in *Hurry On Down* (b) The butts of Jim Dixon's anger in *Lucky Jim*.

Section 4   Did the three writers approve of their 'heroes'?
  (a) Evidence for their approval.
  (b) Evidence for their disapproval.

Conclusion   Who were the 'angry young men', what were they angry about, and what became of them – a summary. The destinies (in brief) of the three writers, and the working-class anger of their successors (Braine, Sillitoe, Wesker).

The essay would thus consist of six parts altogether – though they would not be subheaded as above, nor would they be of equal length. An essay of about 3,000 words is at its most manageable when it is built up of between four and eight parts. Because, again, this essay was to be literary criticism (of a sort) and not social commentary, Sections 1, 3 and 4 would be the biggest – and Section 3 would be the biggest of all.

As Tania read *Hurry on Down*, she made a note of passages like the following (Burge, a middle-class medical student, had been at College with Charles – and it's Burge who's doing the talking):

> *'Just what the bloody hell do you think you're playing at, Lumley, eh? They tell me you've taken a job at the hospital as an orderly. Carrying buckets and emptying bedpans. What the bloody hell's the big idea?' (...)*
>
> *'That sort of work ought to be done by people who are born to it. You had some sort of education, some sort of upbringing, though I must say you don't bloody well behave like it. You ought to have taken on some decent job, the sort of thing you were brought up and educated to do, and leave this bloody slop-emptying to people who were brought up and educated for slop-emptying.'*
>
> Penguin edition, p. 174

It was just this sort of social typecasting that 'the angry young men' were so angry about. Amis's Jim Dixon, for the most part, expresses his 'anger' in Billy Liar-style fantasies. His professor is a bore whom Dixon is obliged to humour if he is to keep his job. The professor is reminiscing, and blocking the path of younger men:

> *'I can remember myself last summer, coming back from that examiners' conference in Durham. It was a real scorcher of a day, and the train was ... well, it ...'*
>
> *After no more than a minor swerve the misfiring vehicle of his conversation had been hauled back on to its usual course. Dixon gave up, stiffening his legs as they reached, at last, the steps of the main building. He pretended to himself that he'd pick*

> up his professor round the waist, squeeze the furry grey-blue waistcoat against him
> to expel the breath, run heavily with him up the steps, along the corridor to the Staff
> Cloakroom, and plunge the too-small feet in their capless shoes into a lavatory basin,
> pulling the plug once, twice, and again, stuffing the mouth with toilet-paper.
>
> Penguin edition, p. 9

There were times when the 'angry young men' wrote more in the style of scarcely grown-up boys, and their anger was an adolescent thumbing of the nose at all authority. This would be one of the points Tania would make in her Conclusion, when the time came to sum up what the anger was about.

Tania would not quote to the extent shown above, even in a 'long' essay. Still, she would quote at greater length than in shorter coursework essays. There (and in the examination), she would 'embed' words and phrases from the texts in her argument, so that every statement she made was grounded in the work under review. In the long essay, she would quote whole sentences and snatches of dialogue, and indent the quotations, and number them, so as to refer to them (by name, and page) in footnotes, or in notes listed at the end of the work.

Final thoughts

I could have gone on to write a sample section, or to tease out the evidence for the three writers' own attitudes towards their heroes (to meet the objectives of Section 4), but 99.9 per cent of you will not be writing long essays about angry young men. It would not have been relevant to your needs, therefore, to go into any more detail. It is hoped that the example given above has been suggestive, and that though Tania's approach to her subject was individual, it is not thought idiosyncratic.

The long essay is the most individual – the most personal – of the coursework demands made on you. It is vital that you be interested in the subject of your investigation, and in its outcome. There should be no question of your taking a title off the peg. Nor will you be left to devise it on your own: it will be a matter for negotiation between you and your teacher, and between your teacher and the moderator. It has to be a study at a recognisably 'advanced' level. But it begins in your own reading – in an author, theme or genre that has meant something to you. If every other examination or coursework text is chosen for you, the two or three texts that you choose to read for the long essay are what should give a coursework syllabus its truly 'alternative' stamp.

INDEX

Abbs, Peter 93–4
Achebe, Chinua 27–8
Albert's Bridge 49
L'Alouette 29
Amis, Kingsley 124–32
Angelou, Maya 92, 105–6
'angry young men' 124–32
Animal Farm 24, 28
Anouilh, Jean 29
Armah, Ayi Kwei 27–8
As I Walked Out One Midsummer Morning 91, 94–5
Auden, W. H. 64–7, 70, 72, 108
Austen, Jane 5, 11–14, 21, 39
Ayckbourn, Alan 37

Barthes, Roland 7
Beckett, Samuel 2, 32, 37
Benedictus, David 99
Bennett, Arnold 119–20
Betjeman, John 60, 61, 66–7, 70, 73, 75
Blake, William 81–4
'Bloomsbury Group' 98, 110
Bolt, Robert 29–30, 37, 49
Bradbury, Malcolm 88
Braine, John 127–8
Brave New World 32
Brooke, Rupert 84–6
Brown, Wayne 75
Brutus, Dennis 75

Calman, Mel 3
Camwood on the Leaves 54–5
Caretaker, The v, 37–9
Carter, Angela 25–6
Catching Them Young: Political Ideas in Children's Fiction 113–15
Causley, Charles 72
Chips With Everything 33–5
Cider With Rosie 91
Color Purple, The 5, 11
Comedians 51–3, 56, 57
Country Wife, The 36–7
Crichton-Smith, Iain 72
Crick, Bernard 90–1, 99
Crucible, The 61–2

Day Lewis, C. 72, 79
Death of a Salesman 40–1
Delaney, Shelagh 33
Devil's Disciple, The 35–6
Dickens, Charles 19–21
Dixon, Bob 113–15
Doctorow, E. L. 1
Drinkwater, John 64, 65
Dubliners 21–3
Dunn, Douglas 78–9
Dylan, Bob 63

Eliot, George 5
Eliot, T. S. 30
Eminent Victorians 98–9
Emma 5
Endgame 32, 37

'Fifty-Minute Hour, The' 3
Figueroa, John 73–4
Fitzgerald, F. Scott 25–6
Forster, E. M. 3, 16–19, 93–4
Fowles, John 6–8
Fox, The 3
French Lieutenant's Woman, The 6–8
Friel, Brian 35

'Garden-Party, The' 14–15
Gardner, Brian 86
Georgian Poetry 67, 84
Go-Between, The 8–11, 12, 27
Golden Gate, The 2
Golding, William 5, 11, 61
Gordimer, Nadine 5, 120
Grass, Gunter 2
Great Gatsby, The 25–6
Greene, Graham 100–2, 107, 108
Griffiths, Trevor 51–3
Gross, John v

Hard Times 19–21
Hartley, L. P. 8–11
Heaney, Seamus 65, 66, 69
Honan, Park 89–90
Hope, Christopher 120–1
Horowitz, Michael 77–8
Hughes, Glyn 72
Hurry On Down 128–32
Huxley, Aldous 32, 108

I Know Why the Caged Bird Sings 105–6
Importance of Being Earnest, The 50–1

James, Henry 3
Jonson, Ben 44–7
Joseph, Jenny 2
Joyce, James 21–3, 83
Jumpers 56–8, 75

Kafka, Franz 5, 93
Keneally, Thomas 27

Lark Rise 102–4
Larkin, Philip 65, 75–9
Lawrence, D. H. 3, 5, 95–7, 120
Leavis, F. R. 5
Lee, Laurie 91, 94–5, 107
Lodge, David 87, 89–90
Long, Michael 43–4
Look Back in Anger 124–32
Lord of the Flies 27
Lucie-Smith, Edward 69
Lucky Jim 128–31

MacBeth, George 79–80
MacNeice, Louis 71–2
Man for All Seasons, A 29–30
Mansfield, Katherine 14–16, 21, 98
Measure for Measure 42–4, 47, 50
Middlepost 88, 120
Midnight's Children 88
Mill on the Floss, The 5
Miller, Arthur 40–1, 61, 62, 66
Morgan, David R. 66
Morgan, Edwin 78
Motion, Andrew 66
'Mr and Mrs Dove' 15–16
Murder in the Cathedral 30

Naipaul, V. S. 74
Ngugi, Wa Thiongo 27–8
Nicholson, Norman 72
Nineteen Eighty-Four 5, 24–7, 40
Northanger Abbey 11–14, 21

Oh What a Lovely War 31
O'Neill, Eugene 119
Orton, Joe 37

Orwell, George   5, 24–5, 40, 90, 113
Osborne, John   124–32
Owen, Wilfred   65, 84–6

Passage to India, A   16–19
Persephone   2
Persuasion   11
Petals of Blood   27–8
Pinter, Harold   v, 37–9, 123–4
Poetry 1900 to 1975   79–80
Pointed Roofs   33
Pound, Ezra   79
Prelude, The   80–1
Pride and Prejudice   39
Priestley, J. B.   37
Pygmalion   35

Rainbow, The   5
Rat, The   2
Richard III   108–10
Richardson, Dorothy   33
Rites of Passage   11
Robbe-Grillet, Alain   7
Romantic Love and Society: Its Place in the Modern World   115
Room of One's Own, A   110–13
Rosenberg, Isaac   84, 86
Rosselli, Amelia   78
Rushdie, Salman   88

Sarsby, Jacqueline   115
Sassoon, Siegfried   79, 84, 86
Satanic Verses, The   88
Scarfe, Francis   71
Schindler's Ark   27
Sea and Sardinia   96–7
Sergeant, Howard   62
Seth, Vikram   2
Shakespeare, William   30, 42–4, 50
Shame   88
Shaw, G. B.   35
Sher, Antony   42, 88, 108–10, 120
Sillitoe, Alan   127–9
Six Feet of the Country   5
Skelton, Robin   70–2
Songs of Innocence and Experience   82–4
Sort of Life, A   100–2
Soyinka, Wole   54–5
Spender, Stephen   72, 79, 107–8
Spire, The   61, 62
Stoppard, Tom   49, 56–8, 75
Strachey, Lytton   93, 98–9

Taste of Honey, A   33
Thomas, Dylan   48–50, 70–1, 77–9
Thomas, Edward   84, 93
Thomas, R. S.   67–9, 77
Thompson, Flora   102–4, 107
Thwaite, Anthony   79

Translations   35
Trial, The   5, 27
Turn of the Screw, The   3

Under Milk Wood   48–50, 54, 57
Unnameable, The   2
Up the Line to Death   86

Vine, Phillip   63
Volpone   44–7

Wain, John   124–32
Walcott, Derek   65, 72–5
Walker, Alice   5, 11
Warner, Marina   87–8
Wasteland, The   79
Weldon, Fay   11, 122
Wesker, Arnold   33–5, 127
What the Butler Saw   37
White Boy Running   120–1
White Stocking, The   62
Wilde, Oscar   50
Woolf, Virginia   33, 93–4, 110–13
Wordsworth, William   80–1
World's Fair   1
Wycherley, William   36–7

Year of the King   108–10